GOD

ON THE INSIDE

I am the good shepherd,
and know my sheep, &
am known of mine....
I lay down my life
for the sheep... there
shall be one fold, &
one shepherd.

John 10: 14-16

Text copyright © Nigel G. Wright 2006
A revised and expanded version of the author's booklet *God on the Inside*, by permission of the
Baptist Union who published the original text in 1990.
The author asserts the moral right
to be identified as the author of this work

Published by
The Bible Reading Fellowship
First Floor, Elsfield Hall
15–17 Elsfield Way, Oxford OX2 8FG
Website: www.brf.org.uk

ISBN-10: 1 84101 484 2
ISBN-13: 978 1 84101 484 5
First published 2006
10 9 8 7 6 5 4 3 2 1 0
All rights reserved

Acknowledgments
Unless otherwise stated, scripture quotations are taken from The New Revised Standard
Version of the Bible, Anglicized Edition, copyright © 1989, 1995 by the Division of Christian
Education of the National Council of the Churches of Christ in the USA, and are used by
permission. All rights reserved.

Scripture quotations taken from the Holy Bible, New International Version, copyright © 1973,
1978, 1984 by International Bible Society, are used by permission of Hodder & Stoughton
Limited. All rights reserved. 'NIV' is a registered trademark of International Bible Society. UK
trademark number 1448790.

Extracts from the Authorized Version of the Bible (The King James Bible), the rights in which
are vested in the Crown, are reproduced by permission of the Crown's Patentee, Cambridge
University Press.

Extracts from The Book of Common Prayer of 1662, the rights of which are vested in the
Crown in perpetuity within the United Kingdom, are reproduced by permission of Cambridge
University Press, Her Majesty's Printers.

A catalogue record for this book is available from the British Library

Printed in Singapore by Craft Print International Ltd

GOD

ON THE INSIDE

The Holy Spirit in Holy Scripture

NIGEL G. WRIGHT

CONTENTS

———— ⁘ ————

INTRODUCING THE THEME

The aim of this book is to expand our understanding of the Holy Spirit and to follow closely the biblical testimony that enables us to do this. Accordingly, the book investigates the person and work of the Spirit in relation to the Godhead, the creation, God's communication with us through inspiration and revelation, the person and work of Jesus the Christ, the Christian life and the future. The book is based on the belief that the Holy Spirit is far more important than most of us realize and that we need to take a fresh look at who the Spirit is and what the Spirit does. We need a larger and more informed understanding of God's Spirit and to recognize the ways in which we are utterly dependent on the Spirit's gracious activity. The title *God on the Inside* is a clear clue concerning the direction we shall take: the Spirit 'searches everything, even the depths of God' (1 Corinthians 2:10). No investigation of the Spirit is adequate which does not recognize the Spirit as active on the 'inside' of God; and, equally, that the Spirit is active on the inside of those who believe and indeed on the inside of creation itself, acting as the Lord and giver of life.

THE NEGLECT OF THE HOLY SPIRIT

Dorothy L. Sayers, the celebrated author and lay theologian, is reputed to have said:

There are those who would worship the Father, the Son and the Virgin Mary; those who believe in the Father, the Son and the Holy Scriptures; those who found their faith on the Father, the Son and the Holy Church, and there are those who seem to derive their spiritual power from the Father, the Son and the Minister!

The implication is that those who truly believe in the Father, the Son and the Holy Spirit and derive their strength from the Three are relatively few. How accurate Sayers was is not a matter that really concerns us. Her statement is true in so far as it points to a widespread ignorance (until more recent times) of the person and work of the Holy Spirit. It is not difficult to see that an imbalance in our vision of God leads to an imbalance in life and a failure to honour the breadth of God's activity.

The Spirit, it has been claimed with some justification, is the neglected member of the Holy Trinity.

When it comes to the Father, there appears to be little doubt about who he is and what he does. The Bible begins with the story of the Creator speaking his powerful word into the cosmos; it continues with the righteous yet merciful God who holds a fallen world together despite its sinful rebellion; it focuses on the electing God who calls Abraham and his descendants to be his people; it magnifies the God who sent Jesus as the world's redeemer.

With Jesus, called the Son of God, there also appears to be little difficulty. Having come from God, he revealed God. He lived among us as the Word made flesh, revealing the Father in his words and actions. The love of God was supremely demonstrated in the sacrificial self-offering of Christ on the cross. In this way, God in Christ reconciled humankind to himself. These wonderful and mysterious realities were made known to us in the resurrection of Christ from the dead, through which Christ was declared to be what he had been from the beginning: the eternal Son of the Father.

As to the Holy Spirit, however, many would be able to echo the words of the Ephesian disciples, 'we have not even heard that there is a Holy Spirit' (Acts 19:2). This may be thought something of an overstatement, and indeed it is. We need to qualify what has been said and in a moment will do so. Nevertheless, until recently, the claim has been substantially true. The Holy Spirit has not been given the necessary attention either in our worship or our thinking.

It may not help that the Holy Spirit can be thought of as 'faceless'. It remains impossible to imagine the Father; it remains true that 'no one has ever seen God' (John 1:18), yet in a way beyond imagination it is possible for us to think of the Father as having a face, a face which is turned towards his children so that he lifts 'the light of his countenance' upon them (Numbers 6:26, BCP). It is also impossible for us really to know the face of Christ, despite the long traditions of Christian art that have depicted him, yet it is certain that God's Son had a face and that those who knew him in his incarnation looked upon him just as he looked upon them (1 John 1:1).

It is also possible, spiritually speaking, for us to behold Christ's face: 'For it is the God who said, "Let light shine out of darkness", who has shone in our hearts to give the light of the knowledge of the glory of God in the face of Jesus Christ' (2 Corinthians 4:6). 'And all of us, with unveiled faces, seeing the glory of the Lord as though reflected in a mirror, are being transformed into the same image from one degree of glory to another, for this comes from the Lord, the Spirit' (2 Corinthians 3:18).

Both Father and Son present themselves to us as distinctive persons united in divine life, yet the Spirit is not to be so imagined. Can we gaze into the face of the Spirit, or is the Spirit to be thought of more as the energy, or the power, or the bond that enables us to look to the Father through the Son, or the force field in which we do this, while remaining himself, or itself, reticent and self-effacing?

REASONS FOR RETICENCE

There are several reasons why the Holy Spirit may have been neglected, among them a biblical reason, a spiritual reason and a theological reason.

A biblical reason

The first reason is rooted in the ancient writings of the Christian faith, which have not only shaped the faith of the Church by their contents but also by the way in which those contents have been narrated and set down. The Bible tells of the unfolding drama of God's dealings with the world. It is progressive in the sense that it moves from promise to fulfilment, from the expectation of God's saving acts in history to the recollection of those acts once they have taken place. It is only in the latter parts of the Bible, particularly in the New Testament, that the Holy Spirit emerges, as it were, most clearly from the shadows into the light of day. This is not to say that the Holy Spirit is unknown or unmentioned in the Old Testament: we will see that this is far from the case. Neither does it mean that the Holy Spirit is inactive until later on: the Spirit is active from the beginning. It certainly does not mean that the Spirit only comes into existence at a certain point of the drama, since the Spirit has always existed and has been at work from eternity. But the full significance of who the Spirit is and what the Spirit does emerges only towards the end of the biblical revelation.

The only proper distinction here is between the 'order of being' and the 'order of knowing'. In the order of being, the Spirit has always existed, but on the level of human knowing, the knowledge and perception of the Spirit's presence are grasped only later. Prominence appears to be given first to the Father (Yahweh) and then to the Son and only then to the Holy Spirit. In the order of God's self-revelation, the Holy Spirit comes into full focus only in the age of the Spirit, which comes later. This explains what is meant by John 7:39: 'Now [Jesus] said this about the Spirit, which believers in him were to receive; *for as yet there was no Spirit*, because Jesus was not yet glorified' (my emphasis). There was 'no Spirit' only in the sense that the age of the Spirit opened up by Pentecost had not yet arrived historically.

It might be seen that the order of this narrative has exerted its influence on the way in which Christians have thought about God for

200 years. Attention has been drawn first to the Father (Yahweh), then to the Son and only then to the Spirit. This is the order of narrative, and narratives shape our perceptions. It is not as though any blame attaches to it: it's just the way the story has worked. Nonetheless, its outcome is an actual neglect of one of the persons of the Trinity and this is bound to have unhelpful consequences.

A spiritual reason

The impression of neglect is heightened when we consider a prime aspect of the Holy Spirit's work. According to Jesus, 'When the Advocate comes, whom I will send to you from the Father, the Spirit of truth who comes from the Father, he will testify on my behalf' (John 15:26). And again, 'He will glorify me, because he will take what is mine and declare it to you' (John 16:14).

This takes us back to what has been said about the 'facelessness' of the Spirit, and here we see the reason for it. It is not the work of the Holy Spirit to draw attention to himself but to Christ, and through Christ to the Father. The Spirit teaches us and enables us to confess that 'Jesus is Lord' (1 Corinthians 12:3). Of course, the work of the Son is to bring us to the Father (John 14:6), so the work of the Spirit is also to teach us through the Son to call God our Father (Romans 8:15–16). The point is that the Holy Spirit is concerned to draw our gaze through the Son to the Father and not to glorify himself. It should not be surprising, therefore, if the Spirit stays somewhat in the background. Indeed, the Holy Spirit has been aptly called 'God in his reticence' (Tom Smail). He does not draw attention to himself but, rather like John the Baptist, points us to the 'Lamb of God who takes away the sin of the world' (John 1:29).

Because this is a spiritual matter and is rooted in the very nature of God's life and being, it is not for mere mortals to question it but to work with it. At the same time, neither should any wrong conclusions be drawn from it, and along the way in this book we shall have occasional reason to point out what some of those wrong conclusions might be. An entirely proper spiritual emphasis on the Spirit's work has sometimes been used as a reason for relegating the Spirit to a place of lesser importance in the life of God. This represents a profound misunderstanding.

A theological reason

Over the years of her history, the Christian Church has attempted to think through what it believes. This attempt to think through its faith is called 'theology'. The essential issues occupied much time and effort in the first centuries of the Church's existence. Having experienced salvation in and through Jesus of Nazareth, the crucial issue was to understand correctly exactly who Jesus was and to express *how* God was present in him, so that certain dangerous misunderstandings could be avoided.

That discussion is not the concern of this particular book. It does indicate, however, that in the history of the Church's thinking the study of the Holy Spirit has taken second place to the study of Christ. In theological language, 'Christology' (the doctrine of Christ) has had priority over 'Pneumatology' (the doctrine of the Spirit). Once more, there are good reasons for this. Everything in Christian faith hinges on our understanding of Christ and it is essential to have this right before moving on to other themes. Indeed, we cannot even understand who the Spirit is unless we first come to terms with Jesus. At the Council of Nicea in AD325, the Church made its decisive statement about Christ by affirming that he was 'of the same substance' as the Father and therefore worthy of equal honour and worship. This was followed in 381 by an equal affirmation about the Spirit. But it can be seen that, for quite valid reasons, reflection upon the Spirit has claimed less attention in the history of the Church than reflection upon Christ.

These three reasons indicate why the Holy Spirit has been neglected in the understanding of the Church. None of them is in itself wrong or sinister. In its own way, each is 'structural'. Honesty compels us to admit, however, that this is not the whole story. At this point we begin to face up to a challenge that will be present throughout this book.

THE LIVING PRESENCE OF THE SPIRIT

The first Christians spoke warmly of the Holy Spirit because for them he was far more than a doctrine. Through the Spirit, the love of God had been poured into their hearts (Romans 5:5). It was through the Spirit that they had first believed, and by his power they had been transformed (for example, Acts 11:1–18). They spoke of the Spirit of God because the Spirit had for them a dynamic, living reality, and they were abundantly conscious of his continuing presence. Nothing can be more obvious: for the early Christians the Holy Spirit was not a theory but a mighty, awe-inspiring and sometimes disruptive power. For them, he certainly was the wind that blows wherever he chooses (John 3:8).

Where this is the case, the Holy Spirit will not be neglected but will be talked about alongside and in unity with the Father and the Son to whom he testifies. Where it is not the case, he will be neglected. People will begin to say again, 'We have not even heard that there is a Holy Spirit.' Our ignorance of the Holy Spirit has more than a little to do with the fact that, unlike the early Christians, many present-day believers have little awareness of the Spirit's presence and power. We cannot rest content with this state of affairs. Unless this book is directed towards the renewal of a true and living experience of God the Father through the Son in the Holy Spirit, it will prove to be of little value. As always, the idea of knowing God carries here far more content than just knowing *of* God. The knowledge of God is personal, existential and experiential as well as intellectual.

At this point we can now qualify the claim that the Holy Spirit has been neglected. From time to time in church history some Christians have emphasized the role of the Spirit, but this emphasis has never been so widespread among the churches as in the last 30 years, when there has been a positive explosion of interest in the Spirit. A neglected area has become a topic on everybody's lips. Several factors account for this, including the charismatic movement, theological questioning and Eastern Orthodox theology.

The charismatic movement

The most obvious factor has been the growth of the charismatic renewal movement. Since the early 1960s, a new awareness of the Spirit and his gifts has been awakened within the historic churches of the Christian denominations and within newer, independent groups. This is a movement of major historical importance. Renewed experience of the Holy Spirit has inevitably led to renewed reflection on him. This has particularly been seen in an examination of the biblical texts (especially 1 Corinthians 12 and 14) referring to the gifts of the Spirit which (it is believed) are being newly appropriated.

Religious historians sometimes distinguish between successive waves of charismatic activity across the 20th century:

- The emergence of Pentecostalism after the Azusa Street, Los Angeles Revival in 1906 involved the rediscovery of speaking in tongues and other 'spiritual gifts'. It led to rapid church growth, especially in South America and Africa, to the extent that Pentecostals now form the largest group within Protestantism. The intense nature of Pentecostal spirituality appears to resonate with the spiritual needs of many ethnic groups and to allow for a freedom of expression that other forms of Protestantism tend to repress.
- In the 1960s, Pentecostal experience of spiritual gifts began to spread to the more historic denominations. When this had happened previously, the mainline bodies proved inhospitable

and new Pentecostal churches separated off to be true to their vision. In the phase of so-called 'charismatic renewal' there was greater success at integrating the perspectives and practices of the renewal movement within the established denominations. At the same time, a more separatist element known as 'Restorationism' looked for a more thoroughgoing reform of church structures and spawned a variety of new 'streams' of churches along the way.

- In the 1980s, a third wave of renewal took place, partly through the ministry of John Wimber and the Vineyard churches associated with him. This phase was characterized by a commitment to 'power evangelism', advancing the Christian ministry through miracles of healing and deliverance, and by unusual phenomena including falling, shaking and other dramatic physical manifestations. In the 1990s, an extension of this phase was seen in the 'Toronto Blessing' (or the 'Toronto Phenomenon', so called by those who were not persuaded that it was much of a blessing).

Each of these movements has had its advocates and its detractors. Part of our concern in this book therefore must be to address the questions raised by the renewal movements and to do so in a way that is fair and balanced. A major concern of this book will also be to show the full range of the Holy Spirit's work, in case we fall into the trap of thinking that one aspect of the Spirit's work is the whole. One danger of the renewal movement is that it might restrict the Spirit's work to one area (specifically Christian experience), while missing altogether the breadth of his activity in other realms, such as in the realm of politics and human society.

Theological questioning

A further factor in the new atmosphere has been a general desire to describe theologically and more fully the manner of God's presence in the world at large as well as in the Church. If the world and all that is in it is truly the Lord's, then we need to find a way of understanding how it is all related to the God who rules and sustains all. This need is made the more obvious because greater awareness of global human experience makes it increasingly difficult for Christians to imagine, as sometimes they have, that God is somehow restricted to the Church. God is Lord of all life, and understanding the Holy Spirit as the one who relates all of life to its source enables us to see not only the Church but all the world in this light.

The last decades have seen a remarkable flowering of Trinitarian thinking in the church and a recognition of the 'promise of Trinitarian theology' (Colin Gunton). It is as though theologians have realized that in the core doctrines of the Christian faith they are in possession of a richer and wiser resource than they had previously been aware. By fully expounding the doctrine of God's unity as Father, Son and Spirit, it has become possible to give more coherent and intelligent accounts of the ways in which Christian thought might meet the challenge of contemporary thought and experience. This is true not least in the ideas of relationship and communion, or community, which are strongly represented in present discourse. When God is understood as a communion of persons in relationship, as is the case in Christian tradition, rather than as a singular ultimate power, as in other forms of monotheism, this doctrine has much to say to a world struggling to realize community not just within the human race but with the whole of a threatened creation.

Eastern Orthodox theology

Openness to Orthodoxy has been a third factor in this reawakened consciousness. Increased interaction with other theological traditions, made possible by the modern world, opens up new avenues. The Eastern Orthodox tradition has tended to place a greater emphasis than Western theology on the Holy Spirit and has been critical of the West for relegating the Spirit to an inferior position within the divine Trinity. In fact, the Great Schism that took place in 1054 between the churches of East and West was ostensibly due to the desire of the

Western Patriarch (the pope) to make a change in the Nicene Creed, asserting that the Holy Spirit proceeded both from the Father 'and from the Son' (*filioque*), a change that the East saw as jeopardizing the status of the Holy Spirit. The more ecumenical and communicative climate of recent years makes it possible to learn from others, and the prominence given to the Spirit in the East is one of the areas where this may happen. The debate is complex. Suffice it to say at this point that, whereas the West has, through the *filioque* clause, linked the work of the Spirit very closely to the saving work of Christ, the East has wanted to conceive of his work more broadly.

Together these factors have created in the last several decades a new climate for examining the person and work of the Spirit of God. This book aims:

- to examine what the Bible teaches concerning the Holy Spirit and to see why it is that the Christian Church has honoured him as the Lord and Giver of Life.
- to seek to understand the full breadth of the Spirit's work within God, the creation, the Church, the Christian believer and human society.
- to explore the best ways in which the work of the Holy Spirit in Christians may be described, so that we may express his work in us and in others accurately and helpfully.

Chapter 1

THE SPIRIT: GOD ON THE INSIDE

This book begins at the end! Rather than collecting all the evidence of what the Bible says about the Spirit and then coming to conclusions about what it means, we will begin with the conclusions already reached by generations of Christians before us. We will then seek to show how those conclusions are justified by testing them against the evidence that the Bible gives.

THINGS MOST SURELY BELIEVED

The Christian Church has affirmed as part of its creed that:

- the Holy Spirit is truly and fully God. The Spirit shares with the Father and the Son the fullness of deity; is not an inferior deity of another kind, nor an inferior part of the one true deity. God's Spirit is fully and truly God, as the Spirit of the Father and the Son in the life of the triune God.
- the Holy Spirit is someone and not something; is not an impersonal force, nor merely the projection of God's power into the world. The Spirit is fully personal and, within the triunity of God, is as personal as the Father and the Son, though in a distinctive way.

In saying these things, any language used of God must be inadequate. It is like trying to capture the immensity of the ocean in a teacup. Yet this is the kind of language that the Bible leads us to use of God. It may be inadequate but it is not inaccurate. It is limited in speaking of the greatest of all mysteries but it is not misleading. This is also the language that we have already seen in the introduction to this book.

We have clearly acknowledged that the Spirit is the Spirit of God and we have used personal pronouns—'he' and 'him'—in preference to 'it'. We have already assumed, therefore, and will go on assuming, that the words of the Nicene Creed are true:

> *And I believe in the Holy Spirit,*
> *the Lord, the Giver of Life,*
> *who proceeds from the Father and the Son,*
> *who with the Father and the Son together*
> *is worshipped and glorified,*
> *who spoke by the prophets.*

This is the faith of the Church. We are beginning at the end in the sense that we are already operating with certain conclusions about the Holy Spirit before we have examined the biblical evidence. It is impossible to avoid this. The large majority of those who read this book will already be committed Christians who gladly affirm the faith that has been handed on to them. But it is necessary to show along the way why these conclusions have been reached and why they are still valid. This will involve examining the witness to the Holy Spirit in the Bible—and that is the task we now begin.

GOD ON THE INSIDE OF THE CHRISTIAN

This chapter is entitled 'God on the inside'. The Holy Spirit is God at work on the inside of the Christian believer. In the words of Tom Smail, he is 'God at his closest to us'. The Father is God above us and over us, 'high and lifted up' (Isaiah 6:1, KJV); the Son is God with us and among us (Matthew 1:23); the Holy Spirit is God in us, on the inside. Jesus said, 'You know him, because he abides with you, and he will be in you' (John 14:17). This is why Paul can say,

'Do you not know that you are God's temple and that God's Spirit dwells in you?' (1 Corinthians 3:16).

Of course, because the Spirit is God's Spirit, this also means that through the Holy Spirit the Father and the Son live within us. Again, Jesus said, 'Those who love me will keep my word, and my Father will love them, and we will come to them and make our home with them' (John 14:23). The Father and the Son come and make their home in Christians through the Holy Spirit: God on the inside. To grasp this is crucial for this reason: what God's Spirit does in the world and in the Church shows us clearly who the Spirit is and what he does *within God himself*. What the Spirit does in believers is characteristic of who and what the Spirit is.

This can be expressed slightly differently along other lines. In 2 Corinthians 13:13 we find the well-known words, 'The grace of the Lord Jesus Christ, the love of God, and the communion of the Holy Spirit be with all of you.' As grace is a prime characteristic of the person and work of Christ, and love is a prime characteristic of the person and work of the Father, so communion or fellowship is characteristic of the person and work of the Holy Spirit. The Holy Spirit creates and produces fellowship. God's Spirit is the bond, the power, that connects each believer with Christ and through him with the Father. Through Christ we have 'access to the Father by one Spirit' (Ephesians 2:18, NIV).

In the same way, the Spirit is the bond between Christians. 'Make every effort to keep the unity of the Spirit through the bond of peace,' says Ephesians 4:3 (NIV). The Spirit is the Spirit of unity, of fellowship; the one who forges relationship. This work is characteristic of what the Spirit is and does in the world, because it is also supremely characteristic of what the Spirit is and does within the very being of the triune God. In other words, what the Spirit does in space and in time reveals what he does in eternity in God. Within God also, the Spirit is the Spirit of communion and fellowship, the dynamic bond of love between the Father and the Son, and much else besides.

GOD ON THE INSIDE OF GOD

Having spoken about the inside of the Christian, is it really possible also to talk about the inside of God? Christians must speak with care and a sense of caution when they attempt to do so. To speak of God 'on the inside' would seem foolish were it not the case that, as we have seen, we have 'access to the Father by one Spirit' (Ephesians 2:18, NIV). It is the privilege of Christians to have access through Christ to the very life of God.

In the Old Testament, the people of God were made aware that they must keep their distance from God. Yahweh's holiness and their sin combined to keep people at a distance. At Mount Sinai the people were warned to keep away from the Lord or 'he will break out against them' (Exodus 19:24). Even when the tabernacle was built, the people were still unable to approach God too closely. Only the high priest was allowed to enter the Holy of Holies and only once a year (Hebrews 9:7–8). The tabernacle and the temple were constructed in such a way as to create a sense of limited access. By means of the temple courts the people were gradually filtered out so that they could approach God on God's terms only, and not without the cleansing blood of sacrifice.

Yet when Jesus made atonement for sins, the curtain of the temple was torn in two (Mark 15:38). In this, a profound spiritual statement is being made. Unrestricted access to God has been opened up for those who believe in Christ. Those who were far away have been brought near through the blood of Christ (Ephesians 2:13–18). Christians therefore have an abundant access to the one they call Father and are able to be bold and confident in making their approach: 'Let us therefore approach the throne of grace with boldness, so that we may receive mercy and find grace to help in time of need' (Hebrews 4:16).

Christians may indeed, therefore, attempt to speak of the inside of God. From the outside, God is one, but those who have been reconciled to God have access to God's inner being. From the inside, we perceive that God is still one, but we understand more about the nature of this unity. It is a unity in variety, a unity of complete communion. God has three ways of being one and the same God. God is God as the Father, as the Son and as the Holy Spirit. The unity of God is a three-dimensional unity. We know this to be so because God has revealed himself in this way and has shown us who he is in his work, in the coming of his Son and the giving of his Spirit. From his work we are able to draw accurate conclusions as to who he is within himself. This 'three-ness' in God is known in the church's language as 'Trinity'.

Perhaps some technical theological language is appropriate and forgivable here. Christian theology has usually made a distinction between the 'economic' Trinity (that is, Father, Son and Spirit as they are seen through their activity in the world) and the 'ontological' or 'immanent' Trinity (that is, God as he is in himself, within his own eternal being). The key point is that the economic and the ontological Trinity are identical. There is not one God at work in the world concealing another God in eternity who bears no relation to the one revealed in time. The way God shows himself in the world is how God actually is in himself. The God revealed in time is a true revelation of the hidden God of eternity. There is no other God apart from this God, who shows himself to be Father, Son and Spirit. Were this not the case, we would not be able to speak of any kind of revelation of God, nor would we be able to rely on the fact that the God who is 'for us' in Jesus (Romans 8:31) is also 'for us' in eternity. This would be a frightening prospect, depriving us of any true knowledge of God. As it is, believing that the eternal God has truly revealed himself in time, we can be assured that the knowledge we have is secure, if by no means complete.

God is a loving community

This understanding of God as divine community is one of the most dynamic and exciting aspects of the Christian faith. It means that, truly understood, God is not some far-off, isolated being. God is a loving community of divine persons who has his being in perfect, self-giving love.

Within God's threefold, three-in-one existence, the Holy Spirit is the Spirit of the Father and of the Son. He is the dynamic, loving bond who expresses and sustains their unity. On the inside of God, the Spirit does the same kind of thing that he does on the inside of, and then between, believers. He creates fellowship. He unites in love. He enables Father and Son to be in perfect harmony with each other in himself. Because he fulfils this purpose first of all within God, the Spirit is able to fulfil the same within those who believe.

DESCRIBING THE SPIRIT'S WORK

These themes have been taken up by many Christian thinkers. We shall look here at one ancient and one modern approach in order to illustrate and expand our thinking on the Spirit.

Augustine (354–430), Bishop of Hippo in North Africa and one of the most influential theologians ever, described the Holy Trinity in terms of Lover, Beloved and Love. By this he meant that the Father is the Lover, the source of love; the Son is Beloved, the one who is loved; and the Holy Spirit is Love, the bond or 'nexus' of love between them. Now it is true, as is often pointed out, that this analogy runs the danger of making the Holy Spirit less than personal. The Spirit might be thought of as a mere bond, the product of two personal agents which is not itself to be thought of in personal terms. It must be borne in mind, then, that the analogy is not a complete and exhaustive one, but in its own way it is attempting to be true to the idea of the fellowship of the Holy Spirit.

Bishop John V. Taylor (1914–2001) developed the theme more recently than Augustine in a famous and elegant book entitled *The Go-Between God* (SCM Press, 1972). The Holy Spirit, according to Taylor, is 'the divine current of communication' between the Father and the Son, eternally holding each in awareness of the other. The Spirit is the 'go-between God', the bond of union between Father and Son, truly God and truly personal, the creator and sustainer of awareness and fellowship not just within God's own being but throughout creation. Similar to Augustine's, Taylor's imagery is also dynamic, living and full of creative possibilities for its application across a wide spectrum of life.

These are helpful trains of thought, not least because they bring God alive for us. God exists in dynamic, creative relationship; he is the living God whose being sparkles and overflows with love and joy. It is this overflow of the divine life that has gone out from God to bring the universe into being and to bring creatures such as ourselves into reconciled fellowship, breaking down the barriers that we erect, filling us also with that fullness of life which is God's own.

So far, so good! But here we come to a major question: have we got it right? Is God really like this? The quick answer is that only God knows! But because Christians believe that God is revealed in Jesus Christ and that the Bible bears witness to this self-revelation, we must go on to ask whether the Bible teaches this understanding of God and specifically of the Holy Spirit. Because our concern is with the Holy Spirit, we will limit ourselves here to examining some of the evidence concerning the Spirit, but we shall find that it connects up with the wider issues.

EVIDENCE FOR THE HOLY SPIRIT'S DEITY

The Holy Spirit is truly God. When we encounter the Spirit, we encounter God in the Holy Spirit and not something other or anything less. The truth of this statement rests on several kinds of biblical evidence, as follows.

The Holy Spirit and God are treated interchangeably. References are made in the New Testament to the Holy Spirit and God in a way that shows them to be interchangeable. For instance,

Acts 5:3–4 records the incident with Ananias and Sapphira. In verse 3, Peter says, 'Why has Satan filled your heart to lie to the Holy Spirit?' and in verse 4 this becomes, 'You did not lie to us but to God.' To lie to the Spirit is to lie to God. Similarly, in 1 Corinthians 3:16 Paul says, 'Do you not know that you are God's temple and that God's Spirit dwells in you?' To be indwelt by the Spirit is to be indwelt by God.

The Holy Spirit is given the attributes of God. Qualities that are ascribed to God are also attributed to the Spirit. These include:

- *power*: 'The Holy Spirit will come upon you, and the power of the Most High will overshadow you' (Luke 1:35).
- *omniscience*: 'For the Spirit searches everything, even the depths of God. For what human being knows what is truly human except the human spirit that is within? So also no one comprehends what is truly God's except the Spirit of God' (1 Corinthians 2:10–11).
- *eternity*: '… Christ, who through the eternal Spirit offered himself without blemish to God' (Hebrews 9:14).

The Holy Spirit performs divine works. The Holy Spirit is said to perform works which are clearly seen to be the works of God. These include creation (Genesis 1:2; Psalm 104:30), the resurrection of Christ (Romans 8:11) and inspiration (2 Timothy 3:16; 2 Peter 1:21). Clearly the Spirit is seen to be the agent of God at work in the world to such an extent as to be equated with God: 'Now the Lord is the Spirit, and where the Spirit of the Lord is, there is freedom' (2 Corinthians 3:17).

In these accumulated texts and verses, the Spirit of God is intimately identified with the whole of God's being and firmly placed on the God side of the divine–human interface. While complete unity is asserted, it is also clear that there is distinction: the Spirit is the Spirit of Christ, but is not Christ; he is the Spirit that comes from the Father, but is not the Father. It is this identity-with-distinction that the doctrine of the Trinity aims to reflect.

EVIDENCE FOR THE SPIRIT'S PERSONALITY

The Holy Spirit is personal. This is not to say that he is a person in the limited and individualist sense that a human being is, but that in the divine manner of being, there is also the kind of personal being and agency of which human being is a mere reflection. Relating to the Spirit, this finds expression in the New Testament in several ways, as follows.

In the use of personal pronouns: In Greek, the word *pneuma* (spirit) is a neuter noun and should take a neuter pronoun ('it'). It is significant, therefore, that on occasions, and in direct defiance of the rules of Greek grammar, the word is actually given a personal (masculine) pronoun ('he'). This is true of John 16:13, 'When the Spirit of truth comes, he will guide you into all the truth; for he will not speak on his own', and probably also of Ephesians 1:14: '… this [who] is the pledge of our inheritance', although here there are two possible readings of the original text. The point is that the rules of grammar have to be bent in order to express the full reality of the Spirit. The rules must be bent in this specific way to be true to the personal nature of the Spirit.

In descriptions of the Spirit's personal role: The Holy Spirit is said to act in ways that are distinctly personal. This is particularly clear in the Gospel of John where, in referring to the Advocate (sometimes also translated as Counsellor or Paraclete) who would come, Jesus says that the Spirit will *teach* and *remind* the disciples (14:26), *testify* (15:26), *convict* the world of sin (16:8) and *bring glory*—but not to himself (16:14). These are all the activities of a personal agent, although sometimes expressed here in the negative mode. The impression is intensified when Jesus makes it clear that his own personal presence with his disciples is continued through the Holy Spirit (14:16–18). It would be impossible to speak in this way of a power that was less than personal.

In the ascription of personal characteristics to the Spirit: The Spirit is spoken of as possessing personal qualities. This is true in the active sense: he is said to possess *intelligence* and *knowledge* (John 14:26), *decision* and *will* (1 Corinthians 12:11) and *emotions* (Ephesians 4:30), the qualities that cumulatively define and describe personal existence. It is also true in the passive sense: the Spirit can be *lied to* (Acts 5:3–4), *grieved* (Ephesians 4:30) and *resisted* (Acts 7:51).

The Spirit is truly personal and truly God. The references cited in support of this are by no means exhaustive, and in the course of this book there will be opportunity to note many others. But enough has been said to confirm the Christian understanding of the Spirit as truly personal and truly God. It comes as no surprise, therefore, to note the outrage felt by Jesus when the works of the Holy Spirit are denigrated: 'Whoever speaks a word against the Son of Man will be forgiven, but whoever speaks against the Holy Spirit will not be forgiven, either in this age or in the age to come' (Matthew 12:32). According to Jesus, to speak against the Holy Spirit is blasphemy. In the mind of the Son of God, the honour of the Spirit of God is of paramount importance.

EVIDENCE FOR THE SPIRIT'S ROLE WITHIN THE TRINITARIAN LIFE OF GOD

Before completing this chapter, we need to review a further area concerning the relationship of the Spirit to the Father and the Son. On two significant occasions the Holy Spirit is mentioned in the closest possible connection with the Father and the Son.

The baptismal formula: In the baptismal formula mentioned in Matthew 28:19, the disciples are commissioned to baptize 'in the name of the Father and of the Son and of the Holy Spirit'. Here are expressed:

- the *unity* of God, since there is one name in which we are baptized.
- the *triunity* of God, since there are three persons within the one name.

- the *equality* of the persons in God, since all three persons are mentioned.
- the *economy* or order within God, since the Father is mentioned first, the Son second and the Spirit third, corresponding to the economy, or order, of God's self-revelation.

The 'grace': In 2 Corinthians 13:13–14 we find the equally well-known words: 'May the grace of the Lord Jesus Christ, and the love of God, and the fellowship of the Holy Spirit be with you all' (NIV). Here also we find the same truths, although expressed differently.

- There is a *unity* of persons, since the divine blessing comes from Father, Son and Spirit.
- There are *triunity* and *equality*, since the persons are each and together the source of divine blessing.
- There is *economy* or order, since the Father is designated as 'God'. This does not deny that Son and Spirit are also God but that the Father is the source of their deity. They have their being from his.

FURTHER INSIGHTS ON THE INSIDE OF GOD

The evidence of the verses above needs to be placed against that of references to the Spirit as the 'Spirit of God' (for example, 1 Corinthians 2:11; Philippians 3:3) and the 'Spirit of Christ' (for example, Philippians 1:19; 1 Peter 1:11). When it is further considered that both the Father and the Son are said to give, send or pour out the Spirit (John 14:16; Acts 2:33), we can see why several further conclusions have been drawn about the relationship between Father, Son and Spirit.

- Because the Father is the Father, he is regarded as the eternal source of the Son and the Spirit. He is, in the traditional language of the church, the 'fountain and origin of deity'.

- Whereas the Son, because he is the Son, may be said (in the words of Nicene Creed) to be 'eternally begotten' from the Father, the Spirit is to be thought of as eternally 'proceeding' or 'going out' from the Father and from the Son. This is suggested by the general way in which the New Testament speaks of the Spirit's work and particularly by the reference in John 15:26 to 'the Spirit of truth who comes from the Father'. Thus the Spirit is not another Son, since the Spirit is not 'begotten'. He has his own unique identity and way of relating within the Trinity.
- Because the Spirit is the Spirit of fellowship, and because he is the Spirit of the Father and the Son, the Spirit may be thought of as the bond of fellowship between Father and Son, the current of loving communication between them.

If these things are true, the picture of God that emerges is exciting: God is the living God, full of life in himself and active among us by his Spirit.

Chapter 2

THE SPIRIT AND CREATION

In Chapter 1 the concern was to understand the Holy Spirit as truly personal and truly God, in other words to establish the most fundamental aspects of Christian conviction about the Spirit and to show how study of the scriptures has led to these beliefs. In the rest of this book we are concerned to understand the breadth and nature of the Spirit's work as it is revealed in scripture. At this point we encounter head-on a difficulty that we will be seeking to address throughout our study.

'YOUR GOD IS TOO SMALL'

Just as Christians can have a God who is too small, so they can have an idea of the Spirit which is too small. We make the Spirit of God too small when, for instance, we restrict the scope of his activity to salvation and to the Church and fail to see the Spirit of God at work in the whole of life. When we do this, we express the mistaken belief that the realm of creation and the realm of redemption are separated off from each other in a dualistic way. The true perspective is that offered in Acts 17:28: 'In him [God] we live and move and have our being.'

These words invite us to see the whole of life, and the work of both creation and redemption, as taking place in God in the sense that 'from him and through him and to him are all things. To him be the glory for ever. Amen' (Romans 11:36). The whole creation is held by the embrace of a gracious God who is the 'Alpha and the Omega, the beginning and the end' (Revelation 21:6). There are no exclusion zones as far as God is concerned and no aspect of life which is not in some way to be related to God.

We need to see first of all that the Holy Spirit is the Spirit of creation. The Spirit is the power of God at work, bringing the world into being and holding it together, and then drawing it towards its destined goal. If the work of the Spirit is particularly characterized by the words 'communion' and 'fellowship', so that he can be called the 'go-between God', it leads us to realize that it is the Spirit of God who holds the world together. He is the power of God present and active in the world. The biblical understanding of creation, then, is as much to do with God sustaining, upholding and acting in providence towards what he has made as with starting the world off in the first place. Our concern in this chapter is 'What is the role of the Holy Spirit in creation?'

To respond to this question, it is possible to proceed in two ways: the way of theological deduction and the way of biblical testimony.

THEOLOGICAL DEDUCTION

It is possible to deduce the role of the Spirit in creation from the statements already made about the Trinity. We have already indicated that although the Spirit comes into true focus only towards the end of the unfolding biblical drama, in the order of being (as distinct from the order of knowing) the Spirit has always existed in the life of God. The Spirit is eternal. Although hidden, therefore, and not always acknowledged in the biblical narrative, we are to understand the Spirit as always present in the activity of God. The work of Father, Son and Spirit in the world should not be divided. What the Father and the Son do is also what the Spirit does; indeed, the Spirit is the agent for their activity. It is essential to recognize that there are distinct relations within the Trinity and that Father, Son and Spirit may be said to fulfil differing and distinctive roles. But when it comes to the work of God in the world, although certain activities are specifically focused in particular persons of the Trinity, the other persons share in those activities as well and are indivisibly co-active in all the works of God in the world.

Thus, although atonement is supremely the work of the Son, it is also the work of Father and Spirit. Although conviction of sin is a work of the Spirit, it would be wrong to say that it is not also the work of the Son and the Father.

When it comes to creation, the work of creation is supremely portrayed in scripture as that of the Father, but in this work the Son and the Spirit share. Putting it slightly differently, if the Spirit really is God, then he must also share in the work of creation since God is the Creator. It should come as no surprise, therefore, to find that the Bible clearly confirms this deduction, as we shall shortly see.

We have not yet finished with our theological deductions, however. There is a further point. In the New Testament, creation is seen as the work of the Father through the Son. The Son of God is spoken of as the Word of God by whom all things have been made. This is particularly clear in John 1:3: 'All things came into being through him, and without him not one thing came into being.'

Christ is therefore the creative word spoken by the Father, and this fits in well with what we read in Genesis 1, the creation narrative, where it is repeatedly recorded in the text, 'And God said…' (vv. 3, 6, 9, 14, 20, 24). God's work of initial creation is portrayed as a process of divine speaking, to which the creation responds in bringing forth new possibilities and realities. But for a word to be spoken, breath is required. Here we see the involvement of the Father in speaking the creative word, of the Son in being the creative word that is spoken, and of the Spirit in being the means (that is, the breath) whereby the creative word is uttered. 'By the word of the Lord the heavens were made, and all their host by the breath of his mouth' (Psalm 33:6).

All this language is, of course, metaphorical but it is as close as we shall come to finding appropriate ideas and images with which to picture the God of biblical revelation. In particular here we notice the close connection between the images of breath, wind and spirit.

In both Hebrew and Greek, the languages of the Bible, these words are one and the same. In using the word 'spirit', neither Old nor New Testament uses capital letters, and the decision to make the word 'Spirit' or 'spirit' in English translations is one made entirely by the translators. The close identity of this group of words, at the least, suggests to us that as breath is essential for life and is close to each one of us, so the Spirit of God is the principle of life underlying the creation and is close to every living being. This leads us to pursue a second path, the way of biblical testimony.

BIBLICAL TESTIMONY

The theological deductions that we have already made from first principles are confirmed by the specific biblical witnesses in a variety of ways. There we are able to find both explicit and implicit confirmation.

Explicit confirmation

A small but significant collection of verses ties the Spirit very closely to creation. For instance, in Genesis 1:2 we find the words, '... and the Spirit of God was hovering over the waters' (NIV). In the NRSV, these words are translated slightly differently as 'a wind from God swept over the face of the waters' and a footnote makes clear that they could also read 'the spirit of God swept over the face of the waters'. This is a case where the one Hebrew word covers all the English possibilities. We are fully entitled here to see a reference to the Spirit of God. Here at the beginning of the creation narrative we are introduced to the Spirit hovering over the formless and empty chaos which has been called into being by God. Out of this raw material the creative word spoken by God then proceeds to shape the ordered world that we know. The implication is that the Spirit is intimately involved in this process. The verb translated 'was hovering' is used in Deuteronomy 32:11 of the eagle fluttering over its young. This suggests something of the attentiveness of God in shaping and forming the creation and doing so through the activity of the Spirit.

The fact that this was indeed the faith of Israel is suggested by Elihu's confession in Job 33:4: 'The spirit of God has made me, and the breath of the Almighty gives me life.' In Hebrew poetry, it is common for the second idea in a sentence to be a repetition of the first in different words. So here we see a parallel between the 'spirit of God' and the 'breath of the Almighty'. The involvement of the Spirit in creation and in the sustaining of all things is also well expressed in Psalm 104:30: 'When you send forth your spirit, they are created; and you renew the face of the ground.'

This involvement of the Spirit extends to the universal presence of God by his Spirit in the world, so that there is no escaping him, nor is there anything hidden from him: 'Where can I go from your spirit? Or where can I flee from your presence? If I ascend to heaven, you are there; if I make my bed in Sheol, you are there… My frame was not hidden from you' (Psalm 139:7–8, 15).

Whenever we make theological deductions it is helpful to find them upheld by specific texts of scripture. In this way we can be assured that the deductions we have made are not wild ones but follow the underlying logic of what is being made known in the scriptures. The texts we have cited give explicit confirmation of the work of the Spirit in creation but there are others that do so in a more implicit fashion.

Implicit confirmation

As noted, in the Old Testament the Hebrew word *ruach* means 'spirit', 'wind' and 'breath'. The word itself occurs 378 times in the Old Testament with at least one of these meanings. In the famous passage about the dry bones in Ezekiel 37:1–14, it is evident that all three possible meanings are being used in close proximity. The wind blows on the bones and puts breath in them, just as the Spirit of God will come upon his people and give them life. In general, it is as if the Spirit is the breath of God activating and moving God's creation, creating and sustaining life: 'In his hand is the life of every living thing and the breath of every human being' (Job 12:10; see also Job 32:8; Genesis 2:7).

The Spirit of God is as essential to life as the wind that blows upon the face of the earth and the breath that activates the living creatures within it. Indeed, the living universe is sustained and upheld from moment to moment by the presence of the creative Spirit who breathes through all creation. The Spirit who is the divine go-between within the Godhead is the same as the relating and connecting power that holds the universe together, the current of communication binding all things together.

All of this points to the closeness of the Spirit of God. It is impossible, with this understanding of the Spirit, to think of God as being distant and far off. The Spirit is as close as the breath or the wind. It is equally impossible to conceive of the Spirit in a narrow or restricted way. The Spirit is in all life and all of creation. Everything that is has its being in God. God's Spirit undergirds and upholds all as the Spirit of life. Whenever we think about the Spirit, we must think big and grateful thoughts.

THE SPIRIT AT WORK IN ALL LIFE

The importance of all this for the Christian should now be clear. As the Creator Spirit, the Holy Spirit is not confined to the Church. It is true, as we shall see, that the Church is in a particular sense the dwelling place of the Spirit, but we must reckon with the Spirit's presence in all the other activities of human life. God's Spirit holds together all the life and all the ways of humankind, even where he is not honoured (Daniel 5:23). This may be summarized in the following section headings, drawing on the witness of the Old

Testament, the understanding of which is essential for the New Testament.

- The Spirit moulds creation and imparts life.
- The Spirit guides the course of nature and history.
- The Spirit enriches human beings with gifts.
- The Spirit bestows on individuals wisdom and leadership abilities.
- The Spirit draws out response to God.

In what follows, I am building in part upon suggestions by James Packer in his book *Keep in Step with the Spirit* (p. 58).

The Spirit moulds creation and imparts life

The Spirit moulds creation into shape and gives life to all created things. Even before the emergence of humankind, therefore, the Spirit was at work in the very fabric of existence. In addition to the texts we have already noted, we might consider Job 26:12–13 as an expression of the faith of Israel: 'By his power he stilled the Sea; by his understanding he struck down Rahab. By his wind the heavens were made fair; his hand pierced the fleeing serpent.'

Specific attention goes here to the 'wind', which can be seen once more as a reference to the Spirit. The poetic language of this particular text is drawn from ancient mythology, in which the chaos out of which creation came is pictured as a sea-serpent. There are echoes here of Genesis 1:1–2, including the reference to the wind or spirit of God, who works to mould creation into a place of beauty.

The Spirit guides the course of nature and history

Writing of the falcons, Isaiah of Jerusalem says, 'Seek and read from the book of the Lord: not one of these shall be missing; none shall be without its mate. For the mouth of the Lord has commanded, and his spirit has gathered them' (Isaiah 34:16).

In asserting the Lord's sovereignty over the nations, Isaiah 40:7 reads, 'The grass withers, the flower fades, when the breath of the Lord blows upon it; surely the people are grass.'

These verses are references both to the involvement of the Spirit within the life of the natural world and to God's providential rule over human history. Nature is itself a realm in which the Spirit of God is active and alive. It is dependent on the continual will of God to uphold the world and grant it life: 'When you hide your face, they are dismayed; when you take away their breath, they die and return to their dust' (Psalm 104:29).

Through the Spirit, God also exercises his rule over the nations so that whatever room God allows for the freedom of both humankind and nature, nothing happens in such a way as to escape the will of God or ultimately to thwart the purpose towards which God is working.

The Spirit enriches human beings with gifts

The Spirit enriches the life of humankind by pouring out his gifts. The Spirit enables creative achievement. There is clear evidence that the creative abilities of humanity should be seen as the gracious gifts of the Spirit of God. For example, in Exodus 31:1–11 and 35:30–35 we read of Bezalel and Oholiab being equipped to construct the Tabernacle and its furnishings:

See, I have called by name Bezalel, son of Uri son of Hur, of the tribe of Judah: and I have filled him with divine spirit [or with the Spirit of God], with ability, intelligence, and knowledge in every kind of craft, to devise artistic designs, to work in gold, silver and bronze… Moreover, I have appointed with him Oholiab son of Ahisamach, of the tribe of Dan; and I have given skill to all the skilful, so that they may make all that I have commanded you.

EXODUS 31:2–4, 6

Much later, after the exile, when the time came to rebuild the temple, the people are reminded through Haggai, 'Work, for I am with you, says the Lord of hosts, according to the promise that I made you when you came out of Egypt. My spirit abides among you; do not fear' (Haggai 2:4–5). These words remind the people that the creative abilities they need for rebuilding the temple remain among them and that by God's grace and gifting they are able to do the work of rebuilding.

Admittedly, these words apply directly to members of the people of Israel but we are not for that reason to think that the Spirit's gifts are only given to the covenant people. If it is true that 'every generous act of giving, with every perfect gift, is from above, coming down from the Father of lights' (James 1:17), then we must apply this across the board. All those skills and abilities that enrich and enhance life, enabling human beings to flourish, must ultimately be referred to God and can be seen to be bestowed by the Spirit.

The Spirit bestows on individuals wisdom and leadership abilities

The idea that the Spirit equips people for leadership emerges as a constant theme in the Old Testament. It is explicitly stated, for example, of Joseph (Genesis 41:38), Moses (Numbers 11:17), Othniel (Judges 3:10), Gideon (Judges 6:34), Samson (Judges 13:25), Saul (1 Samuel 10:10), David (1 Samuel 16:13) and the hoped-for Messiah (Isaiah 11:1–15; 42:1–4). The Spirit who equips for leadership is the Spirit of wisdom and understanding (Isaiah 11:2; Daniel 2:21; 5:14). Certainly, among the people of Israel leadership is seen above all as something that is bestowed by the Spirit, an anointing from God that marks individuals out as exceptionally gifted for the leadership task. It is significant that we refer to some people as being 'charismatic' in their leadership, meaning that an exceptional ability shines through and people are inspired to follow them.

These aspects of the Spirit's work relate to the people of God, so once more it might be thought that they are not evidence of the presence and work of the Holy Spirit to enable creative achievement and bestow wisdom and leadership ability on humankind in general. As the giver of every good gift, it is through the Spirit, the active presence of God in the world, that these gifts must come, and it is certainly true that the people of God are distinct. The prophet Amos makes this point clearly when he gives God's word to the people of Israel: 'You only have I chosen of all the families of the earth' (Amos 3:2, NIV).

It is wrong, though, to assume that the Spirit is restricted to God's people. A later word recorded by Amos reads, '"Are not you Israelites the same to me as the Cushites?" declares the Lord. "Did I not bring Israel up from Egypt, the Philistines from Caphtor and the Arameans from Kir?"' (9:7). God is gracious to all the nations and active by his Spirit within their history, even though this activity may be hidden from us in a way that is not the case with Israel. God holds all the nations within his providential care.

This does not mean, of course, that we should be uncritical or undiscerning. It is clear that the *charism* of leadership in particular is capable of being corrupted and turned to the wrong ends. Abilities, the ultimate origins of which must be ascribed to the grace of God, can nonetheless take their inspiration sinfully and destructively from the dark powers that threaten God's created order. This is reflected in the tragic history of humankind.

The Spirit draws out response to God

The Spirit works to draw out response to God from his human creatures. As we shall see, the supreme work of the Spirit is to bring people to know God through Jesus Christ. This means that the Spirit works to create repentance, faith and obedience—in short, to be the agent of fellowship between God and people.

Primarily we must see this work of the Spirit within his chosen people. The Spirit awakens us to God and causes us to search after him. So the psalmist can say, 'Create in me a clean heart, O God, and put a new and right spirit within me. Do not cast me away from your presence, and do not take your holy spirit from me' (Psalm 51:10–11). Ezekiel and Jeremiah can both point to a new day when the Lord would put his Spirit in his people and cause them to obey him from the heart (Ezekiel 36:24–32; Jeremiah 31:31–34). Furthermore, the Spirit's work in God's people is a prelude to a greater universal work spoken of by Joel:

Then afterwards I will pour out my spirit on all flesh; your sons and your daughters shall prophesy, your old men shall dream dreams, and your young men shall see visions. Even on the male and female slaves, in those days, I will pour out my spirit… Then everyone who calls on the name of the Lord shall be saved.
JOEL 2:28–29, 32

It is through the Spirit, then, that God is at work creating fellowship with people, in his saving purpose first electing Israel and then the Church, in order that through them his purposes of salvation may be extended throughout the world (Isaiah 24:14–16; 1 Peter 2:9–10). The Spirit who breathes through all creation is the one who enables people to respond to the gracious callings of God.

SUMMARY

The object of this chapter has been to broaden our understanding of the Spirit's activity. The Spirit needs to be seen in all of life and all of life needs to be seen in the Spirit. The Spirit is the creating and sustaining power of God. Through him the good gifts of God are imparted to us, enriching life, inspiring creativity, enabling response to God and therefore helping us to find true life as persons made by God and for him.

It is tragically true that humans, as fallen and sinful creatures, have marred the life they have been given and spoiled the creation of which they are stewards. But graciously the Spirit holds us in being, giving us space and time to learn repentance and faith. Our dependence on the Spirit of God is total.

Some reflections on what we have learnt might prove helpful. God is the God of surprises and is to be encountered in places we might not expect. All creation owes its life to God and is upheld by God's power. It is entirely legitimate to see the Spirit of God at work both in the realm of nature and in the various human enterprises by means of which we explore and interpret nature.

Scientists will sometimes speak of nature unfolding its secrets to the humble researcher. Artists will often speak of a sense of inspiration—of something being made known to them as a gift. Many people can speak of moments of revelation and insight coming to them as though from beyond themselves. Whereas we may not wish to interpret all such experiences as being the product of a divine encounter (human beings can be self-deceiving), when they give birth to that which is good, true or beautiful we are entitled to find the Spirit of God at work in these moments.

Theologians sometimes call this God's 'common grace' because it is shown to all: 'But I say to you, Love your enemies and pray for those who persecute you, so that you may be children of your Father in heaven; for he makes his sun rise on the evil and on the good, and sends rain on the righteous and an the unrighteous' (Matthew 5:44–45).

If in one sense God's grace is common, however, in every other sense it is extraordinary and uncommon. To reckon with the presence of the Spirit at work in the whole of life is to open ourselves up to the mysteries of the creation and to the creative journey of discovery in encountering them.

Chapter 3

THE SPIRIT AND REVELATION

In the previous chapter we began to touch on the work of the Spirit in drawing out from people a response to God. The Spirit makes for fellowship between God and people, and acts as the go-between in bringing human beings into communion with God. This reflects and extends the activity of the Spirit between the Father and the Son within the communion of the divine life. Yet it is impossible for such fellowship to become a reality unless human beings see that God exists and that God makes demands on us. Communion with God begins with some kind of perception of God, some way of knowing and seeing the reality of God. It is here, therefore, that we must speak about revelation: the action that God takes to make himself known to us, God's self-disclosure to humanity. The Greek word for revelation (*apokalypsis*) conveys the idea of drawing aside the curtain on what was previously hidden, enabling something to be seen that was previously not seen. Changing the metaphor, it is not only a matter of seeing but of hearing, of blind eyes and deaf ears being enabled both to see and hear.

It is part of the Spirit's work to be the means whereby the word of God comes to us and is heard by us. This is consistent with the understanding we have already outlined of the Spirit as the current of communication between Father and Son. This same Spirit opens up the channels of communication between the Father and our-selves through the Son. It is also consistent with the image of divine speaking that we have encountered in relation to creation. God creates by means of his word; the word spoken in God's creative self-expression is identical with the Son; the means by which the Word which is the Son is uttered is the breath or Spirit of God. The Spirit is intimately associated with revelation and inspiration, and the Spirit's involvement in the work of revelation is the subject to which we now turn.

THE SPIRIT AND PROPHECY

The fact that the Holy Spirit enables people to speak from God is a clear theme in scripture. It is most obvious in 2 Peter 1:21: 'No prophecy ever came by human will, but men and women moved by the Holy Spirit spoke from God.' The sense here is of being carried along by a wave or by the wind, and this is not an inappropriate way of describing the prophetic experience in both Old Testament and New Testament. It takes varied forms as God speaks 'in many and various ways by the prophets' (Hebrews 1:1).

We shall examine at this point the witness of both Testaments, and then proceed to explore the experience of prophecy today.

The Old Testament

From early on in Israel's history, the Spirit was associated with prophecy. So we read of Balaam, 'Then the Spirit of God came upon him, and he uttered his oracle' (Numbers 24:2–3). When the time came to anoint Saul as king over Israel, Samuel told him that, in confirmation, he would encounter a procession of prophets and 'the spirit of the Lord will possess you, and you will be in a prophetic frenzy along with them and be turned into a different person' (1 Samuel 10:6).

This early prophetic dynamic became characteristic of the later movement in which the prophets interpreted the ways of God to the covenant people. In the case of Ezekiel, the revelation of God came both in vision and word (see Ezekiel 2:2; 3:12–14; 11:1, 5, 24; 37:1). The prophet proclaims in Isaiah 61:1, 'The spirit of the Lord God is upon me, because the Lord has anointed me; he has sent me to bring good news to the oppressed, to bind up the broken-hearted, to proclaim liberty to the captives, and release to the prisoners.' These words are echoed by Micah: 'But as for me, I am filled with power, with the spirit of the Lord, and with justice and might, to declare to Jacob his transgression and to Israel his sin' (3:8).

It was the Holy Spirit, then, who impelled the prophets to be bearers of the word of the Lord. The Spirit enlightened their minds to perceive in the events of history a depth of meaning hidden from others. Through dreams and visions they perceived what was in the heart of the God of the covenant, and the Spirit pressed the work of the Lord on them with such urgency that they were compelled to speak. They were 'carried along by the Holy Spirit' (2 Peter 1:21, NIV).

The New Testament

Against this Old Testament background, it comes as no surprise to find similar prophetic experiences in the New Testament. In the tradition of the Old Testament prophets, the word of God came to John the Baptist (Luke 3:2), a man who 'even before his birth [would] be filled with the Holy Spirit' (Luke 1:15). With prophetic insight, John saw the Spirit of God descending and resting on Jesus (John 1:33). After his baptism, Jesus himself entered into a prophetic ministry in fulfilment of the words from Isaiah already quoted: 'The Spirit of the Lord is upon me...' (Luke 4:18–19; compare Isaiah 61:1–2). He is later described as 'Jesus of Nazareth, who was a prophet mighty in deed and word before God and all the people' (Luke 24:19).

On the day of Pentecost, Peter saw the fulfilment of the prophecy of Joel concerning the outpouring of the Spirit in the last days:

In the last days it will be, God declares, that I will pour out my Spirit upon all flesh, and your sons and your daughters shall prophesy, and your young men shall see visions, and your old men shall dream dreams. Even upon

my slaves, both men and women, in those days I will pour out my Spirit;
and they shall prophesy.
ACTS 2:17–18; COMPARE JOEL 2:28–32

The church after Pentecost was marked by this prophetic constraint,
the urge to prophesy. We read of the prophet Agabus, who proclaimed,
'Thus says the Holy Spirit…' (Acts 21:10–11), a New Testament
equivalent of the Old Testament prophetic formula, 'Thus says the
Lord'. The prophetic experience was in evidence in Corinth and was
seen by Paul as a gift of the Spirit to be desired because of its usefulness
in building up the people of God (1 Corinthians 12:7–11; 14:1–5).
The prophecies of John the Seer were given in visions when he was 'in
the spirit' on the Lord's day (Revelation 1:10).

From this selection of evidence we are able to see that the Spirit
brings to God's people the revelation of God. The Spirit is the means
by which God gives himself to his people, enabling them to know
what is in his heart and mind. There is something about the Spirit
that heightens our perceptions of God and God's purposes, which
gives depth to the ways in which we understand and interpret the
world. The Spirit brings understanding to our minds and a sense of
vitality and urgency to our feelings. At this point, people will often
speak about the 'quickening' of the Spirit. The word is instructive.
Originally it is drawn from the idea of 'enlivening' (as in the Prayer
Book phrase 'the quick [meaning the living] and the dead'), but
experience of the Spirit can be in the form of a quickening of our
perceptions and of our emotions, so that we feel as if we are being
'speeded up', grasping truths with a new urgency and concern. All of
this is part of being carried along by the Spirit and acting under the
Spirit's influence and constraint.

The prophetic today

How might all of this be expressed in the contemporary church, if at
all? There are some who believe that the prophetic belongs

exclusively to the world of the Bible and that we are neither to look for such experiences today nor to believe those who claim to have them.

In one sense, this must surely be right. The scriptures are the 'canon' or measuring rod by which all claims to spiritual experience must be tested, and no one has authority either to take away from scripture or add to it (Revelation 22:18–19). If any prophets or teachers claim to speak with authority equal to that of canonical scripture, then this is a sure sign that they are false. The only proper approach is that of humble submission to the guidance and rule of Christ mediated through the biblical testimony, and all attempts to contest that authority are suspect, whatever impressive and dramatic signs may accompany them (Deuteronomy 13:1–5). But the normative word of God found in scripture needs to be applied in every generation, with wisdom and insight, to situations that we encounter which may not themselves be anticipated in scripture.

It is at this point, in the application of the canonical word to contemporary reality, that we need to look for prophetic inspiration. Here we can be assured that the Spirit of prophecy continues to come to the aid of God's people. We may perhaps see this at various levels.

The level of expository preaching: Expository preaching consists in wrestling with the scriptures so that we are able, in whatever format, to speak again into our reality the word that once was spoken in scripture. It is as if, within all the texts and passages of the Bible with all their varied contexts and diverse forms, a word waits to be discerned and delivered once more into our world. This is a skilled task and requires the ability to understand the Bible accurately and interpret it faithfully. But most of all it requires a willingness to be inspired by the Spirit in first listening to the scriptures and then rendering them as a word for today.

Few preachers are strangers to the sense of being carried along by the Spirit in this task, and most will be able to recognize the moments when, either in the preparation or the delivery of a word from God, there is an added urgency and authority in what is preached. The Spirit then enables people to connect with what is said and to receive it as a word for themselves. It is as though the word of God in that moment becomes God speaking directly to us in a way that transforms us.

The level of personal encouragement: Much of what is called 'prophecy' today might better be understood as exhortation (Romans 12:8; 1 Corinthians 14:3). In other words, it is the application of general truth about the love and purposes of God to individual needs and circumstance. There is no doubt that this can be very helpful.

A slightly different experience would be the discerning and affirming of gifts, opportunities or guidance for a given individual. It ought to be clear that for anyone to presume to speak to another in the name of Christ or the Holy Spirit is a very weighty thing and should only be done with care and sensitivity. There is no shortage of stories about people making wild claims or pronouncements concerning others, which can be singularly unhelpful and mis-leading. However, where there is a desire to encourage and build up, where the words that are offered to an individual are clearly biblical and Christian, and where whatever kind of guidance or prediction is offered tentatively and for further testing, this too can be a helpful form of ministry.

The level of strategic mission: 1 Chronicles 12:32 records the case of the people of the tribe of Issachar 'who had understanding of the times, to know what Israel ought to do'. This is another level of prophetic insight, discerning what is appropriate for the times in which we live, in serving the mission of God on which we are sent. While it should be understood that in Christ and the scrip-tures we have an abiding and reliable access to the truth about God and God's purposes, the ways in which that truth relates to the particulars of our own day and age require interpretation and application, which in turn require the inspiration of the Spirit.

In this sense we might be able to see in Dr Martin Luther King an example of a contemporary prophet. Rooted in the scriptures and their vision of God's justice for all people, he burned with indignation at the treatment of his own people in the segregated South of the United States in the mid-20th century. He was able to speak powerfully into his generation, to galvanize a movement for change that has had immense consequences. Here we are no longer in the realm of prophetic words being spoken in the church to build up individuals and strengthen them (valid as this is), but in the realm of hard social and political reality, in ways that closely parallel the ministries of the greatest prophets such as Isaiah, Ezekiel and Jeremiah.

One more word is appropriate here. The three levels of contemporary prophecy outlined above suggest ways in which the Spirit of God might be seen to be active in today's world. In the wake of the charismatic movement, it became common to hear people prophesying using the formula 'Thus says the Lord...' or using direct personal speech such as 'I the Lord say to you...'. How should we reflect on these usages?

One reflection would be that even when the central message of a prophecy might be deemed to be inspired by the Holy Spirit, it is often packaged in a form of words that is learnt from the religious group to which a person belongs. In some circles, for instance, it is clear that the preferred style for prophecy is definitely King James Version! These are learned styles rather than part of the inspired message, and those who aspire to prophesy do well to distinguish the difference.

A further reflection would be that if it is a weighty thing to believe that we have a word from God, it is even more weighty to speak as though we are God, in the form 'I, the Lord, say to you...'. Experience suggests that even this is part of the learned style rather than the essential message of prophetic utterances, and whereas we could not say that it is always wrong, we might assert that it is somewhat risky to put oneself in God's place. A first-person message can be delivered equally effectively in the more modest third-person mode, in which we speak about God rather than as God.

In summary, under the authority of Christ mediated in scripture, there is a place not for the statement of new versions of the truth but for new applications of that truth. This application normally comes through preaching but may also come in exhortations addressed to individuals and in the ability to discern the times. However it is expressed, it is advisable to avoid an overdramatic style and to speak humbly and modestly, always allowing those who receive the words the freedom to test them and judge whether they are truly from God. It is not the mode of their delivery but the validity of their content that determines whether they are truly prophetic.

THE SPIRIT AND SCRIPTURE

An extension of the Spirit's inspiration of prophecy is the inspiration of scripture. The scriptures are, in large measure, the collected oracles of the prophets or prophetically edited writings interpreting Israel's history or, in the case of the New Testament, writings interpreting Christ and his work. Within the variety of scripture there are, however, writings that fit readily into none of these categories but are nonetheless preserved as scripture because they have some witness to offer about the ways of God with Israel and humankind, or about the nature of human response to that witness. In the Bible, the inspired words of prophets and apostles become 'inscripturated' (that is, written down as scripture) in such a way as to enable them to be preserved, to be disseminated and to function as a common authority given in the life of the whole Church to inform, guide and direct the Church's life.

Speaking with reference to the Old Testament, 2 Timothy 3:16–17 asserts, 'All scripture is inspired by God and is useful for teaching, for reproof, for correction, and for training in righteousness, so that everyone who belongs to God may be proficient, equipped for every good work.' These words have commonly been extended to the New Testament on the basis of John 14:26 and

16:13, where Jesus tells the apostles that the Spirit will guide them into all truth. When these verses are combined with 1 Corinthians 2:13, where Paul claims to have taught the truth in 'words... taught by the Spirit', the conclusion is that both Testaments are the inspired word of God.

Literally translated, the word 'inspired' is 'God-breathed', and is a claim that the final origin of the scriptures, beyond the many people who played their part in the writing and editing of the actual text, is to be found in God. This means that there is no need to play down the roles played by the authors and compilers of the documents. Inspiration is not dictation in the way in which Muslims, for example, conceive of the Koran being given through Mohammed. It is a more complex and mysterious process by which, under the guidance of the Spirit, the writings emerged in their present form. As the Spirit was at work inspiring the prophets, so he was at work calling into being the scriptures as we now possess them. Inspiration therefore says something about the way in which these writings have come to be and about the one from whom they ultimately come.

There is also, however, something here about the very nature and content of what is written. There is a spirituality to the biblical writings. God by his Spirit has invested himself in the words of scripture, so that they bear witness to the central Word which is Jesus Christ himself (Luke 24:25–27; John 5:39–40). Those who step into the world of the Bible and engage with the things of which it speaks become part of the story. There is an energy within these writings so that they can be described as 'divinely spiritual'. They make their impact upon individuals and communities. The creative power they mediate is one that will not finally be controlled by any human power or agency. They speak to the human situation in ways that are ever new and fresh. The word of God is 'living and active, sharper than any two-edged sword, piercing until it divides soul from spirit, joints from marrow; it is able to judge the thoughts and intentions of the heart' (Hebrews 4:12).

The result of the Spirit's activity is that the Bible we now possess is 'useful for teaching, for reproof, for correction, and for training in righteousness' (2 Timothy 3:16). Implicit in this is the fact that the scriptures, by reason of their inspiration, are altogether reliable in fulfilling their central purpose, bearing witness to Jesus Christ and awakening people to living fellowship with God when they are made to live by the Spirit.

The prophets and apostles of Old and New Testaments, who were inspired by the Spirit of God and taught the ways of God accurately, continue to guide the Church because the words that they spoke and the teaching they gave lives on for us in the holy scriptures. As the Spirit carried them along and enabled them to bear their witness, so the same Spirit has sustained their words in written form and continues to breathe upon them so that they live for us today.

This brings us to the next area for investigation.

THE SPIRIT AND ILLUMINATION

A word spoken but not heard does not profit us. In a sense, what we have said about the source of prophecy and scripture in the Spirit stresses the objective side of revelation: the Spirit has spoken through individuals in space and in time and has preserved their testimony in the classic writings of the Bible. These writings now constitute a 'given', an external authority that needs to be acknowledged throughout the Church and which we are not at liberty to tweak in any direction we choose. They have their own integrity, and justice demands that we deal with them as they are, with all their angularity as well as all their glory, rather than manipulating them to say what we wish to hear.

This objectivity is only part of the movement of the Spirit of God towards us in revelation, however. The word spoken must be 'heard'; that which is revealed must be 'seen'. Breakthroughs need to happen in the realm of perception, in the subjective dimension in correspondence to the objective realm. Something must take place in us to complete the movement of God towards us in revelation; otherwise revelation hangs in the air without fulfilling its goal of creating fellowship between God and persons. This 'something' is the work of illumination. This also is the Spirit's work, most clearly spoken of in 1 Corinthians 2:9–16, of which the following words are a part:

'What no eye has seen, nor ear heard, nor the human heart conceived, what God has prepared for those who love him'—these things God has revealed to us through the Spirit; for the Spirit searches everything, even the depths of God… Now we have received not the spirit of the world, but the Spirit that is from God, so that we may understand the gifts bestowed on us by God… 'For who has known the mind of the Lord so as to instruct him?' But we have the mind of Christ.

Paul makes it clear that this revelatory work comes through the words that are given by the Spirit in person and spoken in the apostolic preaching. Although not accepted by a person who does not have the Spirit, those who do have the Spirit (spiritually minded believers) accept the words for what they are (vv. 13–16).

It is evident, then, that the Spirit who knows the fullness of God invests himself in the words of the apostolic preaching, in order to give himself through them to those who receive the word. Those who receive the word have their minds illuminated by the Spirit. This corresponds with what Paul has said elsewhere:

I pray that the God of our Lord Jesus Christ, the Father of glory, may give you a spirit of wisdom and revelation as you come to know him, so that, with the eyes of your heart enlightened, you may know what is the hope to which he has called you, what are the riches of his glorious inheritance among the saints, and what is the immeasurable greatness of his power for us who believe, according to the working of his great power.
EPHESIANS 1:17–19

There is such a thing as saving knowledge, and in the experience of salvation there are things that every person needs to know. This is not the secret knowledge prized by the movement known as Gnosticism, which arose during and after the New Testament period —a knowledge accessible only to an initiated élite. Instead, it is the open knowledge that has been 'publicly exhibited' in Christ (Galatians 3:1), the significance of which was perceived by the disciples through the Spirit. It is the truth as heard, seen, observed and touched by the apostles in Christ (1 John 1:1–4).

It makes sense to say that the Spirit who creates fellowship, the divine current of communication, the go-between God, should be involved at both ends of the revelatory process. The Spirit is involved in the speaking and the hearing, the showing and the seeing. The Spirit enables revelation both to happen and to be received. The Spirit is in the drawing near of God to people and of people to God. The Spirit crosses the divide between the two, and in such a way as to lead us to confess that all is of God's grace. The Spirit is able to reveal God because he himself is God. The Spirit is able to illuminate persons and interact with them because he himself is personal.

With these things in mind, it now becomes essential to show how the Spirit who breathes through all creation and reveals God to humanity cannot be thought of without reference to Jesus Christ.

—— Chapter 4 ——

THE SPIRIT AS THE GIVER
OF JESUS

We have taken note of the role of the Spirit in imparting revelation. It is crucial to add that the supreme revelation of God is given in the person of Jesus Christ. That is why Christ is recognized as the Word of God who was with God in the beginning, who became a human being, and who makes the God whom no one has ever seen known in visible form (John 1:1, 14, 18). As the writer to the Hebrews explains, God may have spoken 'to our ancestors in many and various ways', but in the last days he has spoken by a Son who is both the 'heir of all things' and the one 'through whom he also created the worlds'. This Son can be the supreme revelation because he is 'the reflection of God's glory and the exact imprint of God's very being' (Hebrews 1:1–3). Properly speaking, the revelation which is the content of scripture is Jesus Christ. The Hebrew scriptures look forward to his coming in anticipation and the Greek scriptures look back to his coming in recollection. Christ is the Word of God who is contained in scripture and was made flesh as Jesus of Nazareth. He is God speaking to humankind.

Once more, however, we must recognize the relationship between the Word that is spoken and the breath by which it is spoken. If the Spirit is the Spirit of revelation, then the Spirit must be supremely engaged in enabling the revelation to be made manifest through Jesus Christ. As in Hebrew the word *ruach* means 'breath', 'spirit' or 'wind', so in Greek the word *pneuma* can also mean 'breath', 'spirit' or 'wind'. As the creative word of God was uttered by the Spirit at the beginning of time, so the revelatory and redemptive Word which is Jesus Christ was spoken or impelled into human history by the Spirit of God.

Again we come to a crucial point that expands our understanding of the Spirit. Our inclination is to think of the Spirit as having been sent into the world by Christ. This is true and is explicitly stated by the apostle Peter on the day of Pentecost: 'Being therefore exalted at the right hand of God, and having received from the Father the promise of the Holy Spirit, he has poured out this that you both see and hear' (Acts 2:33). This may, however, obscure for us the equally important truth that the Son of God has come into the world through the Holy Spirit. The Spirit has given us Christ before Christ has given us the Spirit. The gift of Christ comes to us from the Father by the Spirit.

In this chapter we trace this theme. Our concern is to show that it is by the Holy Spirit that the Word has become incarnate; it is by that same Spirit that the particular human identity of Jesus of Nazareth has become the bearer of the eternal Son of God. It is by the Spirit that Christ has lived out his life in obedience to the Father and given himself up in saving sacrifice for the world. The whole life and ministry of Jesus is to be attributed to the work of the Spirit within him. In support of this claim, we notice in the biblical account of Christ the following aspects of the Holy Spirit's work:

- The Spirit prepared the way for the coming of Emmanuel.
- The Spirit entrusted the Son of God to the womb of Mary.
- The Spirit empowered the life and ministry of Jesus Christ.
- The Spirit enabled the sacrificial self-offering of Jesus.
- The 'Spirit of holiness' raised Jesus to life in the resurrection.

THE SPIRIT PREPARED THE WAY FOR
THE COMING OF EMMANUEL

The observation that the Spirit opens up the way for the coming of Jesus is particularly noticeable in the Gospel of Luke. Suddenly, after years of God's apparent silence and the absence of prophecy, a flurry of spiritual activity breaks out. It begins with the promise of a son to Zechariah and Elizabeth. It is as if the barren years are past, the days of fulfilment have arrived and a day long awaited has now arrived. Of the son to be born (John the Baptist) it is said, 'Even before his birth he will be filled with the Holy Spirit' (Luke 1:15). Shortly afterwards, the angel-messenger appears to Mary and she receives the promise that 'the Holy Spirit will come upon you, and the power of the Most High will overshadow you' (1:35). When Elizabeth meets her cousin Mary, Elizabeth is filled with the Holy Spirit and pronounces a blessing on her (1:41–42).

Mary herself, in an experience reminiscent of ecstasy in the Old Testament, is inspired to utter a psalm of praise to God as her spirit 'rejoices in God my Saviour' (1:46–55). A similar experience engulfs Zechariah when John is born: 'His father Zechariah was filled with the Holy Spirit and spoke this prophecy...' (1:67). Among other things, Zechariah prophesies that his son will be a prophet of the Most High (1:76). Of John himself it is said that he grew 'and became strong in spirit' (1:80).

After the birth of Jesus, his parents are blessed by a righteous and devout man, Simeon. It is recorded that 'the Holy Spirit rested on him. It had been revealed to him by the Holy Spirit that he would not see death before he had seen the Lord's Messiah' (2:25–26). This revelation was fulfilled when, 'guided by the Spirit, Simeon came into the temple'. There he encountered Mary and Joseph and their child and blessed them with inspired words (2:26–32).

These brief pictures create an impression of a devout group of Jewish believers being prepared by the Spirit to receive the Messiah for whom they had hoped. Jesus is born into a circle of people who represent the best of Jewish devotion and in whom the fire of Old Testament faith is kept burning. It is not that the Holy Spirit has been absent and then returns, but that in such a remnant as this the work of the Spirit is very much a living reality. God does not abandon his world, but even as it resists him he prepares it quietly and secretly to receive the one who will redeem it. So here we have the Spirit preparing the way for the coming of Immanuel, God with us, to comfort and redeem his people (Matthew 1:22–23). The one who had inspired the prophet to speak of his coming (Isaiah 7:14) watches over his word to bring it to fulfilment (Jeremiah 1:12).

THE SPIRIT ENTRUSTED THE SON OF GOD TO THE WOMB OF MARY

Jesus was conceived in Mary's womb through the action of the Spirit. She is told, as we have noted, 'The Holy Spirit will come upon you, and the power of the Most High will overshadow you; therefore the child to be born will be holy; he will be called Son of God (Luke 1:35). This promise is given while Mary is yet 'a virgin engaged to a man whose name was Joseph' (Luke 1:27).

The idea that the 'power of the Most High' will overshadow Mary is instructive here. It is reminiscent of the Spirit who hovered over the waters at the time of creation (Genesis 1:2), and who now hovers over Mary to do a new work of creation in her womb. Equally, it recalls the idea of the cloud, the symbol of the divine presence, which covered the tent of meeting so that 'the glory of the Lord filled the tabernacle' (Exodus 40:34). Christ was to be the new temple, the one in whom God was present among his own people and in whom his glory would be displayed (John 1:14). It happened therefore that 'when [Jesus'] mother Mary had been engaged to Joseph, but before they lived together, she was found to be with child from the Holy Spirit (Matthew 1:18). Joseph was told in a dream, 'The child conceived in her is from the Holy Spirit. She will bear a son, and you are to name him Jesus, for he will save his people from their sins' (Matthew 1:20–21).

It was through the Spirit that the Son of God became incarnate in the womb of a virgin. This 'virgin birth' or (more accurately) 'virginal conception' is a sign of the action of God through the human being, Jesus of Nazareth. The creative Spirit, who overshadowed the waters at the birth of creation, here overshadows a young Jewish girl to perform in her womb, and with her willing co-operation, a gracious, creative miracle. It is a miracle of new creation. The one to be born is given in order to renew a fallen race and to recreate the purpose of God. Into the old world is born the agent of the new world, and the Spirit who was present at the birth of the old is present at the birth of the new in the midst of the old. Moreover, he is the active power that brings both to pass.

Jesus' humanity is taken from his mother Mary, and as one 'born of a woman' (Galatians 4:4) he has a complete human nature and identity. Yet Jesus Christ is not the product of the human race, not even of the most devout Jewish members of it. He is the product of the recreative power of God, working sovereignly within humanity by his Spirit to bring to birth a new people. By the Spirit, God causes one to arise from within Israel who will be the anointed Messiah of God and will redeem his people.

THE SPIRIT EMPOWERED THE LIFE AND MINISTRY OF JESUS CHRIST

Jesus was born of the Spirit in order to live in the Spirit. We find therefore that 'the child grew and became strong, filled with wisdom; and the favour of God was upon him (Luke 2:40; compare Isaiah 11:1–3). At the age of twelve he amazed the teachers in the temple with his understanding (Luke 2:46–47, see also v. 52). This was a sign of the Spirit resting upon him.

It was, however, with his baptism that Jesus entered into the fullness of his mission. This baptism is recorded in all four Gospels as the time when 'the heaven was opened, and the Holy Spirit descended on him in bodily form like a dove' (Luke 3:21–22; see also Matthew 3:16–17; Mark 1:10–1). In the Gospel of John, this occasion was the moment when John the Baptist recognized the fulfilment of a revelation given to him by God: 'He on whom you see the Spirit descend and remain is the one who baptizes with the Holy Spirit' (John 1:33).

This verse expresses more fully the crucial role of Jesus. The Spirit descended on Jesus at his baptism, not because the Spirit was previously absent but to inaugurate the age of messianic fulfilment and to anoint Jesus for the ministry into which he now entered as the Messiah. Jesus was the one who came to overcome evil and set people free from the dominion of darkness. In the whole of his ministry and then through his death and resurrection, Jesus was becoming the one who would mediate between God and humanity. He was to be the one who baptizes in the Holy Spirit, through whom the Spirit is mediated to bring the age of salvation and new life to sinners.

After his baptism, the Spirit remained on Jesus and enabled him to fulfil the mission for which he had been sent into the world. Jesus, full of the Spirit, was led by the Spirit to be tested in the wilderness (Luke 4:1). Having proved more than equal to the test, he returned from the wilderness in the power of the Spirit (Luke 4:14) and proclaimed his new awareness of his mission in the synagogue at Nazareth:

The Spirit of the Lord is upon me, because he has anointed me to bring good news to the poor. He has sent me to proclaim release to the captives and recovery of sight to the blind, to let the oppressed go free, to proclaim the year of the Lord's favour.
LUKE 4:18–19

According to the picture presented by the Gospels, Jesus now exhibits a profound consciousness of the Spirit of God. He hears the Holy Spirit speaking in the Old Testament scriptures (Matthew 22:43–44), understands his mighty acts of power as being accomplished by the Spirit of God (Matthew 12:28), and accuses those who denigrate his works of blaspheming against the Holy Spirit (Matthew 12:31; Luke 12:10). He casts out demons 'by the finger of God' and sees in these signs the fact that the kingdom of God has come to people (Luke 11:20). He speaks to the disciples of the willingness of the Father to give the Holy Spirit to those who ask (Luke 11:13), assures them of the fact that the Holy Spirit will help them when they are on trial (Luke 12:12), and commands them to baptize in the name of Father, Son and Spirit (Matthew 28:19).

A fascinating and unusual glimpse is given into the inner life of Jesus' beliefs and convictions in Luke 10:21–22. Very rarely are we privileged to see what takes place in the emotional life of Jesus, but here we read:

At that same hour Jesus rejoiced in the Holy Spirit and said, 'I thank you, Father, Lord of heaven and earth, because you have hidden these things from the wise and the intelligent and have revealed them to infants; yes, Father, for such was your gracious will. All things have been handed over to me by my Father; and no one knows who the Son is except the Father, or who the Father is except the Son and anyone to whom the Son chooses to reveal him.'

Here we see the Spirit as the one who causes joy to well up in the heart of Jesus, overflowing in thanksgiving and praise and expressing the intimacy of the relationship of the Son with the Father who is Lord of heaven and earth. We see here Jesus' awareness of his unique Sonship and his sense of the mission on which he has been sent, to become the mediator between God and humankind of the knowledge of God which he himself enjoys.

Central to all of this is the Spirit who joins the Father to the Son and is the wellspring of the Son's worship of the Father. In John 4:23–24, Jesus says, 'The hour is coming, and is now here, when the true worshippers will worship the Father in spirit and truth, for the Father seeks such as these to worship him. God is spirit, and those who worship him must worship in spirit and truth.' If this is true, then Jesus is the prime exemplar of true worship. He worships the Father by the Spirit, rejoicing in the intimate relationship that exists between himself and the one who is Lord of heaven and earth. In this experience we might see the Spirit once more as the divine current of communication between the Father and Son, a relationship that exists in eternity but is expressed here in time, between the one in whom the Son of God has come to us and the eternal Father.

It is clear, then, that we are unable to understand either the life or the mission of Jesus other than as absolutely dependent on the Spirit. The Spirit of God is the activating power within Jesus, as was later recalled by Peter: 'That message spread throughout Judea, beginning in Galilee after the baptism that John announced: how God anointed Jesus of Nazareth with the Holy Spirit and with power; how he went about doing good and healing all who were oppressed by the devil, for God was with him' (Acts 10:37–38).

But this is not all.

THE SPIRIT ENABLED THE SACRIFICIAL SELF-OFFERING OF JESUS

We have already drawn attention to the words in John 1:33 that point to Jesus as the one who both receives and imparts the Holy Spirit. Christ is the one who will baptize with the Holy Spirit. It is significant that these words occur immediately after John the Baptist's reference to Jesus as 'the Lamb of God who takes away the sin of the world' (1:29). The link is important. It is by taking away the sin of the world that Christ can mediate the Holy Spirit to those who believe.

Even here, in the self-offering of Jesus, the work of the Holy Spirit is to be recognized, although it is explicitly spoken of on only one occasion in the New Testament. That occasion is in Hebrews 9:13–14:

For if the blood of goats and bulls, with the sprinkling of the ashes of a heifer, sanctifies those who have been defiled so that their flesh is purified, how much more will the blood of Christ, who through the eternal Spirit offered himself without blemish to God, purify our conscience from dead works to worship the living God!

These words will recall the servant of the Lord spoken of in Isaiah 42:1: 'Here is my servant, whom I uphold, my chosen, in whom my soul delights; I have put my spirit upon him; he will bring forth justice to the nations.' This is the servant who is then portrayed in Isaiah 53:12 as the one who 'poured out himself to death'. As the Spirit enabled the self-sacrifice spoken of in Isaiah 53, a self-sacrifice that brought justice to the nations, so in Hebrews 9:14 it is the eternal Spirit who enables Jesus to offer himself as both priest and victim to cleanse his people. The Spirit is the motivating and enabling power behind the self-offering of Jesus throughout his life and then supremely in his death.

We should not overlook the Hebrews reference to the Spirit as 'eternal'. As we have noted, eternity is an exclusive property of God, and its application to the Spirit here is a confirmation of the Spirit's divine status.

If we are able confidently to identify the Spirit at work in the atoning death of Christ, it is difficult to penetrate beyond this point and ask what the Holy Spirit was doing when the Son of God gave himself over to death and experienced abandonment at the cross. We deal here with holy mysteries, concerning which the New Testament itself says little, if anything. Yet perhaps it may be claimed that as the Son of God journeyed into the darkness of death, as he 'tasted death for everyone' (Hebrews 2:9), he was accompanied on his way by the Holy Spirit in order that the Spirit might retrieve him from death. Some would see a hint of these mysterious events in 1 Peter 3:18–20:

For Christ also suffered for sins once for all, the righteous for the unrighteous, in order to bring you to God. He was put to death in the flesh, but made alive in the spirit, in which also he went and made a proclamation to the spirits in prison, who in former times did not obey, when God waited patiently in the days of Noah, during the building of the ark, in which a few, that is, eight people, were saved through water.

If this is indeed a reference to what the Son of God was doing in between dying and being raised, then the reference to being 'made alive in the spirit' is not without significance. It is the Spirit of God who is the agent of being made alive in this way: there can be no other such source. The Spirit who accompanied Jesus was able to be the agent of the next moment in the earthly existence of the Son of God.

THE 'SPIRIT OF HOLINESS' RAISED JESUS TO LIFE IN THE RESURRECTION

According to Romans 1:4, Christ 'was declared to be the Son of God with power according to the Spirit of holiness by resurrection from the dead'. The 'Spirit of holiness' is an alternative way of referring to the Holy Spirit. The Spirit was the active power behind the raising of Jesus. 1 Peter 3:18 asserts, 'He was put to death in the flesh, but made alive in the spirit', which could equally be translated as 'made alive by the Spirit'. With even greater clarity, Romans 8:11 proclaims, 'If the Spirit of him who raised Jesus from the dead dwells in you, he who raised Christ from the dead will give life to your mortal bodies also through his Spirit that dwells in you.'

If it is correct to understand the Spirit as accompanying the Son of God on his journey into the abandonment of death, it is surely by that same Spirit that the Son is retrieved from death and raised to new life. We may see in this the fulfilment of the words quoted by Peter on the day of Pentecost: 'For you will not abandon my soul to Hades, or let your Holy One experience corruption. You have made known to me the ways of life; you will make me full of gladness with your presence' (Acts 2:27–28; compare Psalm 16:8–11).

It is by the Spirit that Christ is preserved from corruption and restored to new life. Once more, the Spirit, designated by the Nicene Creed as 'Lord and Giver of Life', is associated with the bringing of life just as at the dawn of creation. But now this is life of a whole new order. Jesus is not just restored to mortal existence but taken beyond it into the realm of the glorious future life that is God's ultimate goal for his creatures. God's grace is now revealed 'through the appearing of our Saviour Christ Jesus, who abolished death and brought life and immortality to light through the gospel' (2 Timothy 1:10).

SUMMARY

By now it should be clear that Jesus Christ has indeed come to us by the Holy Spirit. The Spirit prepared the way for his coming, caused him to be conceived in Mary's womb, enabled and empowered his ministry, was the means of his sacrificial self-offering at the cross and restored him to a new dimension of life by the resurrection. Jesus Christ is the supreme gift of God by the Holy Spirit to this world.

The role of the Holy Spirit in the activating and inspiring work of the incarnation is one that has been generally overlooked. In formulating a doctrine of the incarnation, the tendency has been to stress what is called a 'Word-Christology'—that is to say, one that majors on the idea of the Word becoming flesh in a downward movement from God into humanity. Debates around this subject have concerned themselves with questions such as how the divine attributes of omnipresence, omniscience and omnipotence can be reconciled with the limitations of existence as a human being.

What has been described in this chapter, however, might be named a 'Spirit-Christology' in that it focuses upon the role of the Holy Spirit as the means whereby the eternal Word was joined to a single human identity in incarnation. The stress is on the dependence of the human being Jesus on the Holy Spirit by whom were conveyed to him all the divine resources he needed to fulfil the mission on which he was sent. In this understanding, there is no need to account for a limitation on the divine nature in Christ's becoming human. The glory of the incarnation is precisely that Christ does come from God in humility and weakness, but aided in his mission by the Spirit of God. As a human being, Christ fulfils the vocation of humanity—to live for God's glory alone. As a human being representing all humanity, he makes atonement for our sins and offers to the Father a life of obedient love, so fulfilling on our behalf all that is required of us. In doing this, Christ manifests the Father's omnipotence in that even in this way, through weakness, suffering and death, he is able to achieve the divine purpose. This is a manifestation of the divine wisdom that rules and guides all things. Far from the incarnation being some kind of denial of God's eternal power and wisdom, it is precisely the highest manifestation of both.

This Spirit-Christology is not meant to suggest that Jesus was merely the most Spirit-filled man who has ever lived. He was that, but more besides. It was through the Spirit that the eternal Son of God was joined to a distinct and individual human personality. Through the Spirit, human nature was rendered capable of bearing in incarnation the eternal Son of God, in such a way as to present us with the one human person, Jesus of Nazareth, who is fully God and fully man. Properly speaking, therefore, this is more than a Spirit-Christology. We might best describe it as a trinitarian Christology, which gives full expression to the involvement of Father, Son and Spirit in the work of incarnation. The Father sends the Son into the world by means of the Spirit. By the breath which is the Spirit, the Father utters the Word of God in the form of human life and flesh, in order that human beings may see, know and be saved. The Spirit is the giver of the Christ. For this inexpressible gift, and for the giver of the gift, we are eternally grateful to the triune God.

Chapter 5

THE SPIRIT AS THE GIFT OF JESUS

Now we turn the tables. The Spirit is the giver of Jesus and is also the gift of Jesus. Jesus comes to us by the Spirit and the Spirit comes to us by Jesus. This is what is indicated in John 1:33: 'He on whom you see the Spirit descend and remain is the one who baptizes with the Holy Spirit.'

This verse captures the theme perfectly. The Spirit descends and rests on the Christ in order that he might become the very one through whom the Spirit is then mediated in power to others. It is now our task to explore this theme.

THE SPIRIT: THE GIFT OF JESUS TO HIS CHURCH

In Acts 2:33 the apostle Peter declares concerning the risen Christ, 'Being therefore exalted at the right hand of God, and having received from the Father the promise of the Holy Spirit, he has poured out this that you both see and hear.' The dramatic events of the day of Pentecost recorded in Acts 2 are understood as the 'outpouring ' of the Spirit by Christ upon the Church, the Church's baptism in the Holy Spirit as foreseen and prophesied by John the Baptist. The Spirit comes as the mighty wind (v. 2) and with tongues of fire (v. 3) to fill the waiting believers. All this is interpreted as the fulfilment of the prophecies of Joel concerning the 'last days' (v. 17). The 'last days' have arrived because the Christ of God has come and has brought to fulfilment in his life, death and resurrection the eternal purpose of God. Anything that follows these events of ultimate significance must be seen as 'the last days', however long that period lasts.

In referring to the coming of the Holy Spirit, Peter refers to the things that the disciples 'both see and hear'. In some sense, Pentecost is a visible and audible event, just like the blowing of the wind: the wind can be heard and its effects can be seen. Pentecost is strangely reminiscent of the activity of the Spirit in the Old Testament, as the Spirit overwhelms the disciples and causes them to speak in other tongues (v. 4), to behave (apparently) like drunken men (v. 13) and to testify with great boldness to Jesus Christ (vv. 11, 14–36). It may be compared with the experiences of Saul in 1 Samuel 10:5–11, in which he is caught up into the spiritual enthusiasm of a band of prophets and himself begins to prophesy, being turned into a different person. We are told, 'The spirit of God possessed him, and he fell into a prophetic frenzy along with them. When all who knew him before saw how he prophesied with the prophets, the people said to one another, "What has come over the son of Kish? Is Saul also among the prophets?"' (vv. 10–11).

Some would resist the idea that Pentecost was an event of such spiritual enthusiasm and intensity, but the evidence suggests that it was a dramatic occasion accompanied by unusual happenings which caused startled comment. It is important to note that this incident is interpreted by Peter as the gift of the promised Spirit from the ascended Christ. It may be seen, therefore, as the initial fulfilment of Luke 3:16, 'He will baptize you with the Holy Spirit and fire', and Acts 1:5, 'John baptized with water, but you will be baptized with the Holy Spirit not many days from now'. It is clearly implied in Acts 2:33 that, now the Christ is exalted, he is in a position to fulfil the promise of the Old Testament and of his own ministry by pouring out the Spirit.

This link between the gift of the Spirit and the work of Christ is also indicated in John 7:37–39:

'Let anyone who is thirsty come to me, and let the one who believes in me drink. As the scripture has said, "Out of the believer's heart shall flow rivers of living water."' Now [Jesus] said this about the Spirit, which believers in him were to receive; for as yet there was no Spirit, because Jesus was not yet glorified.

According to the Gospel of John, the lifting up of Jesus on the cross, his resurrection and ascension are to be understood as the glorifying of Jesus (John 17:1–5). Through cross and resurrection, the glory of Jesus is revealed. The clear implication is that, before the Spirit can be given as the permanent and abiding presence of God within his people, the work of Christ as the sacrificial Lamb of God must be fulfilled. He must die, rise and ascend, completing his earthly ministry and opening up the way to the Father for those who believe, so that the life of God may be poured upon them in the Spirit. Once this reconciling work is accomplished, the Spirit who has been promised may be given.

Christ, as God incarnate and now as the risen Lord, becomes the mediator of the Spirit to those who are his. This does not imply that the Spirit was previously absent from the world. We have already seen that the Spirit is the active presence of God within the created sphere. But it does imply that, because of Christ's reconciling work, there is a new mode of the Spirit's presence. The Spirit is present not just as Creator-Spirit but as Redeemer-Spirit, indwelling those who believe and opening up an abiding fellowship with the Father through the Son. What began with the day of Pentecost is a new age, the age of messianic fulfilment, when the identity of God's Messiah is known and the blessings of his reign can be received.

It is no coincidence that, in origin, Pentecost was a harvest festival, the feast of Weeks, which celebrated the end of the grain harvest (Leviticus 23:15; Deuteronomy 16:9). It occurred fifty days (which is what 'Pentecost' means) after Passover. With Pentecost, the time of ingathering begins as the gospel is preached to diverse ethnic groups within Judaism (Acts 2:9–11) and they are enabled to hear it in their own languages as the disciples speak in tongues given by the Spirit (2:3–4). After the preaching of the gospel, more than three thousand people are won to faith in Christ as the firstfruits of the great harvest that is now to be gathered, with others following on a daily basis (2:41, 47).

The actual event of Pentecost is described as 'a sound like the rush of a violent wind' in which 'divided tongues, as of fire' rest on the disciples (2:2–3). Both images resonate with the Old Testament, in which the powerful wind, understood to be under God's control, is frequently referred to, as we have seen (see also Exodus 10:13; Psalm 18:42). Fire is often associated with the presence of God and God's holiness in the Old and New Testaments (Exodus 3:2; 13:21–22; Hebrews 12:29), and with the purification that God brings to human lives (Revelation 3:18).

When John 7:39 affirms, 'For as yet there was no Spirit, because Jesus was not yet glorified', it points not to the non-existence of the Spirit before this time but to the decisive coming of the Spirit in a new way. The Spirit whom the first believers came to experience as their companion and guide was not known in this way until after the ministry of Jesus was complete. This new mode of the Spirit's presence is indicated in John 14:17, where Jesus says, 'This is the Spirit of truth, whom the world cannot receive, because it neither sees him nor knows him. You know him, because he abides with you, and he will be in you.'

As the gift of Jesus, therefore, the Spirit opens up a new world for those who are Christ's. The Spirit is known by believers in a way that is not true of those beyond the family of faith, even though the Spirit is the one who holds their lives together and bestows gifts and graces upon them. In the Christian community, the Spirit is known consciously and specifically. Up until Pentecost, the disciples of Jesus had known the Spirit as one who was with them—as indeed was true of the people of God of the Old Testament, who experienced the Spirit's equipping and anointing from time to time. From the coming of the Spirit at Pentecost, however, the Spirit was to be 'in' the disciples, permanently indwelling their lives and remaining in them so that they could become the dwelling place of God.

It is with this new world that much of the rest of this book is concerned, and the following point is crucial for our understanding of that new world.

THE SPIRIT: THE CONTINUING PRESENCE OF JESUS CHRIST IN THE WORLD

The Spirit is now the continuation of the presence of Christ in the world without limitations of space or time. This is what Jesus taught his disciples. He first of all told them, 'I will ask the Father, and he will give you another Advocate, to be with you for ever', and later added, 'Nevertheless, I tell you the truth: it is to your advantage that I go away, for if I do not go away, the Advocate will not come to you; but if I go, I will send him to you (John 14:16; 16:7).

These are highly significant words for understanding the Spirit and his present work. Jesus teaches that the Spirit is 'another Advocate'. The word here translated 'advocate' is more literally translated as 'paraclete' and carries the meanings of 'encourager' or 'comforter'. The word 'counsellor' is used in the RSV and NIV to hold all these meanings together. Just as Jesus has been with his disciples, encouraging and guiding them and interpreting to them his teaching, so when he is gone they will not be left as orphans: the Spirit of truth will lead them into truth (John 16:13), and will support and encourage them. The Spirit will be with them as an advocate when they are put on trial (Matthew 10:19–20; Mark 13:11).

Literally, 'paraclete' refers to one who is 'called alongside' to help. In 1 John 2:1, the same word is used of the ascended Christ who represents us to the Father. John 14:16 highlights the fact that the Holy Spirit is *another* advocate. In Greek, as in some other languages, there are different words that can be translated into

English by the word 'another'. One word means 'another of a different kind' and a further one means 'another of the same kind'. The word used here implies that the Spirit is another of the *same kind* as Jesus himself. This is highly significant in establishing the divine status of the Holy Spirit: once it is agreed that Christ shares the Father's divine nature, it follows that the Holy Spirit also does, since the Spirit is of the same kind or the same nature as the Christ. Indeed, the Holy Spirit is the one through whom Christ continues to be present with his own people and can be thought of as Christ himself in a new form: 'Now the Lord is the Spirit, and where the Spirit of the Lord is, there is freedom' (2 Corinthians 3:17). This is why, in John 14:18, Jesus can say, 'I will not leave you orphaned; I am coming to you'.

The Spirit is Christ himself, present in a different form. There is an identity between Christ and the Spirit, and at the same time a difference, since the Spirit is *another* Advocate. Here once more we have the mystery of the Holy Trinity, the unity in distinction in God. The persons of the Holy Trinity are distinct but united; they may be said to indwell each other and so to experience a complete unity. As God is spirit, this mutual indwelling is complete and perfect. When Jesus prayed for his disciples and those who would come to believe through them, he prayed, 'As you, Father, are in me and I am in you, may they also be in us, so that the world may believe that you have sent me' (John 17:21). Human beings may experience something like the unity that is in God, but only God knows it in perfection. Because of the mutual indwelling of the persons of the Trinity, wherever the Spirit is active the Father and the Son are also active in what the Spirit is doing. The Spirit is the extended presence of the Father and the Son, God going out from God's own self to be with and among God's own people.

This helps us to understand a second point about the teaching of Jesus.

THE SPIRIT'S COMING IS FOR OUR OWN GOOD

The presence of Jesus through the Spirit is to our advantage: 'It is to your advantage that I go away, for if I do not go away, the Advocate will not come to you' (John 16:7).

Here, Jesus' 'going away' refers to his journey to the cross and to death, and beyond that to the Father's presence through resurrection and ascension. By this going away, which demonstrates that his earthly mission has been accomplished, Jesus makes possible the coming of the Spirit. The Spirit's coming is to the disciples' advantage precisely because the presence of Christ with his people is no longer limited in space and time by the conditions of the incarnation. Christ is now universally present by the Spirit who knows no bounds and who can reach into all corners of the earth. Christ can also promise therefore always to be with the disciples (Matthew 28:20) because by the Spirit his personal presence is made universally real. The Lord is the Spirit. As Christ was in flesh and blood the Emmanuel, the one in whom God was with us, so now he continues to be God with us to the ends of the earth, with all power and authority given to him. The disciples of Christ therefore have an immense advantage—the abiding and continuing presence of their Lord in every situation and circumstance.

To think of the Spirit in this way opens up new depths to the hope of Christ's second coming. It is customary to refer, by means of this term, to the final coming of Christ in glory, along the lines suggested immediately after the ascension: 'Men of Galilee, why do you stand looking up towards heaven? This Jesus, who has been taken up from you into heaven, will come in the same way as you saw him go into heaven' (Acts 1:11). The point is further amplified in Hebrews 9:28: 'So Christ, having been offered once to bear the sins of many, will appear a second time, not to deal with sin, but to save those who are eagerly waiting for him.'

Yet these verses are referring to the visible and public return of Christ: 'Look! He is coming with the clouds; every eye will see him, even those who pierced him; and on his account all the tribes of the earth will wail' (Revelation 1:7). The New Testament records for us two other ways in which we might think of the coming of Christ, not publicly to all but specifically to his disciples after his death. One form of his coming is the resurrection itself, in which Christ is restored to his followers; a further form is his coming through the Spirit at Pentecost. It is possible, therefore, to think of Christ's coming in glory as threefold: in the resurrection, in the Spirit at Pentecost, and then finally and publicly in his coming to judgment and to final vindication.

The idea that we should think of Pentecost as a coming of Christ by means of the Spirit is suggested by other verses. In John 14:1–3 we read:

Do not let your hearts be troubled. Believe in God, believe also in me. In my Father's house there are many dwelling-places. If it were not so, would I have told you that I go to prepare a place for you? And if I go and prepare a place for you, I will come again and will take you to myself, so that where I am, there you may be also.

Granted that these words of Jesus are often read as a reference to his second coming, or to the experience of death (which is why they are frequently used at funeral services), they may also refer to the living communion with Christ that is our possession now by the Spirit.

Then there are the words in Matthew 16:27–28:

For the Son of Man is to come with his angels in the glory of his Father, and then he will repay everyone for what has been done. Truly I tell you, there are some standing here who will not taste death before they see the Son of Man coming in his kingdom.

These words have puzzled people for many years, as they specifically seem to claim that some of Jesus' hearers would still be alive when the 'Son of Man'—Jesus in his glorified state—came a second time.

If this is what Jesus had in mind, some have concluded, then Jesus must have been mistaken, since all who heard him speak are long since dead. However, if we see that the Son of Man 'comes' in his resurrection and then in the Pentecost event, and then finally, visibly and publicly, in the 'second coming' in the fullness of time, the words of Jesus make sense as they stand. Some who heard him would indeed see him coming in resurrection and at Pentecost as the glorified Son of Man bringing God's kingdom.

At Pentecost the one who comes is the Spirit of Jesus Christ, who continues and expands the presence of Christ in the world, in the community that recognizes him as the Messiah of God.

THE SPIRIT'S COMING IS ABIDING AND PERMANENT

Jesus' teaching tells us that the Spirit is with God's people for ever. 'And I will ask the Father, and he will give you another Advocate, to be with you for ever' (John 14:16). The presence of the Spirit, as the one in whom Christ abides with his people, is to be permanent.

Here we have a major and important difference between the work of the Holy Spirit in the Old and New Testaments. It is intriguing to ask what exactly the difference might be between the people of God in the Old and those in the New. It is certain that the saints of the Old Testament knew and loved God, and this could only be the case if they had experienced the grace of regeneration, being made alive to God inwardly by the Spirit. Although they did not know the name of Christ, they were able to call on the name of the Lord (Yahweh) and to receive from him forgiveness for their sins (Psalm 31:17, 91:15, 145:18). In these respects they were in no way at a disadvantage to Christians in the New Testament, but in another sense they were at a disadvantage, since certain things were hidden from them and were revealed only with and through the coming of Christ: '"What no eye has seen, nor ear heard, nor the human heart conceived, what God has prepared for those who love him"—these things God has revealed to us through the Spirit' (1 Corinthians 2:9–10).

The difference between the Old and the New, however, consists not so much in the nature or quality of individuals' experience of God as in the age in which they were living. The Old Testament era was a time of expectation and anticipation, whereas the New Testament is concerned with the age of prophetic and messianic fulfilment. The Old Testament looked forward to a time when God would act in a new way:

A new heart I will give you, and a new spirit I will put within you; and I will remove from your body the heart of stone and give you a heart of flesh. I will put my spirit within you, and make you follow my statutes and be careful to observe my ordinances. Then you shall live in the land that I gave to your ancestors; and you shall be my people, and I will be your God.

EZEKIEL 36:26–28

Although the people of Israel did indeed return from exile, they never experienced the fullness of what was promised and continued to look forward to a time of spiritual renewal. It was this time that came with Jesus and led to the coming of the Spirit at Pentecost.

In the Old Testament, the Spirit came on individuals for specific tasks and functions and then departed. In the New Testament, the Church knows the Spirit as a permanent, indwelling reality that characterizes the whole of its life and ministry. The Spirit does not depart from God's people but continues among them. There are indeed times when the Spirit equips for particular tasks (as we shall see), but he also resides permanently and continually in the Church and makes Christ present for ever in and among his people. In the Old Testament, the Spirit dwelt in the tabernacle and then the temple in the midst of the people. In the New Testament, the Spirit dwells within the people themselves, who therefore become the very temple of the living God for which tabernacle and temple were preparations (1 Corinthians 3:16–17; 2 Corinthians 6:16; Ephesians 2:21).

It is for this reason that the Spirit is the gift of Christ to his Church. He bestows upon God's people permanent fellowship with the Father in the Son.

THE SPIRIT WORKS TO GLORIFY CHRIST

The Holy Spirit is at work in the Church, bringing its members into a full realization of what has been done for them and given to them in Jesus Christ. This is shown by the words of Jesus: 'He will glorify me, because he will take what is mine and declare it to you. All that the Father has is mine. For this reason I said that he will take what is mine and declare it to you' (John 16:14–15).

Jesus Christ is God's last word, so the Spirit is not to be understood as superseding Christ in any way, as though in the age of the Spirit Jesus Christ is no longer necessary or of interest. This is a cast of mind that some people have occasionally embraced, as though by going beyond Christ to the Spirit they were progressing from the earthly to the heavenly, or the lower wisdom to the higher wisdom. But because Christ is the Son of God, it is impossible to supersede him. Revelation or wisdom can never rise higher than the Christ 'in whom are hidden all the treasures of wisdom and knowledge' (Colossians 2:3). This is because, in Christ, 'all the fullness of God was pleased to dwell' (Colossians 1:19) and the fullness of our life is in him.

What is needed is not in any way to go beyond Christ, but to go more deeply into the knowledge of God of which he is the mediator. The work of the Spirit, therefore, is not to surpass Christ but to take us into the fullness of Christ, to enable us to see and experience the knowledge that the eternal God is here for us in Christ and that we will never exhaust him. The Spirit draws our attention to Christ; he focuses on Christ; he causes us to see again and again that 'what has come into being in him was life, and the life was the light of all people' (John 1:3–4). 'From his fullness we have all received, grace upon grace. The law indeed was given through Moses; grace and truth came through Jesus Christ' (John 1:16–17).

This aspect of the Spirit's work has been aptly called 'the floodlight ministry' (J.I. Packer). The beauty of a building can be brought out and enhanced by well-designed floodlighting, placed in such a way as to capture architectural details that might otherwise escape the eye. In his book *Keep in Step with the Spirit*, Packer has expressed it as follows:

When floodlighting is well done, the floodlights are so placed that you do not see them; you are not in fact supposed to see where the light is coming from; what you are meant to see is just the building on which the floodlights are trained. The intended effect is to make it visible when otherwise it would not be seen for the darkness, and to maximise its dignity by throwing all its details into relief so that you see it properly. This perfectly illustrates the Spirit's new covenantal role. He is, so to speak, the hidden floodlight shining on the Saviour… The Spirit, we might say, is the matchmaker, the celestial marriage broker, whose role is to bring us and Christ together and ensure that we stay together. As the second Paraclete, the Spirit leads us constantly to the original Paraclete, who himself draws near… through the second Paraclete's coming to us.

The floodlight ministry is not the whole of the Spirit's work. We have already seen many other dimensions and shall go on to take note of others. But this is indeed the central facet of the Spirit's work and is consistent with all that we have so far covered. If the Spirit is the breath that enables the creative and redemptive Word to be uttered, then it is that same Word that the Spirit speaks into the lives of individuals today. This is how the Spirit's work is to be recognized. Any spirit (teaching, ideology, truth claim, religious experience, fashion or whatever) that does not point to Christ, is inconsistent with him or claims to go beyond him to some other fountainhead, is not the Holy Spirit, the Spirit of Christ.

Beloved, do not believe every spirit, but test the spirits to see whether they are from God; for many false prophets have gone out into the world. By this you know the Spirit of God: every spirit that confesses that Jesus Christ has come in the flesh is from God, and every spirit that does not confess Jesus is not from God. And this is the spirit of the antichrist, of which you have heard that it is coming; and now it is already in the world.
1 JOHN 4:1–3

It would be a mistake to assume that because the Spirit's prime ministry is to glorify Christ, the Spirit is therefore lesser in importance or status than Christ. Quite the opposite is true. It is *because* the Spirit glorifies Christ in this way that the Spirit is to be honoured among Christian people. Jesus himself found that there were some places, such as his own home town, where the people did not honour him and, as a consequence, 'he did not do many deeds of power there, because of their unbelief'. The experience prompted him to exclaim, 'Prophets are not without honour except in their own country and in their own house' (Matthew 13:57–58).

By derivation we must say that where the Spirit is not honoured, the Spirit is not free to fulfil the mighty work of glorifying Christ. Those who seek to glorify Christ do well to honour the Spirit. This in itself means honouring the Holy Spirit as God. A mistaken belief is that because the Holy Spirit does not glorify himself but Christ, we should not seek to honour or glorify the Spirit in our worship. This is a wrong and unfortunate deduction. *Because* the Spirit shares equally in the divine nature, and *because* the Spirit is reticent about himself for the sake of bringing glory to Christ, it is entirely right to worship the Spirit along with the Son and the Father. This truth is well borne out in the hymns and liturgies of the Church in which this is consistently done, and rightly so, since God—Father, Son and Spirit—is to be worshipped.

In exploring the theme of the Spirit as the gift of Jesus, we have attempted to understand the relationship between the exalted Christ and the outpoured Spirit. Through the Spirit, Christ is personally present with his people. The Spirit leads the Church into that life which is ours in Christ, drawing our attention to him. The Spirit prompts the confession that 'Jesus Christ is Lord' (1 Corinthians 12:3).

We will now go on to explore how the Spirit fulfils his work in the Church as a community and in the individuals who are its members.

Chapter 6

THE SPIRIT AND THE CHURCH

The Church of Jesus Christ is the community of the Holy Spirit. The Church came into being as a direct consequence of the coming of the Holy Spirit and continues to exist in the power of that same Spirit. It is notable that among the many images of the Church to be found in the New Testament, the three predominant images are trinitarian: the Church is understood as the people of God, with its ultimate origin in the will and purpose of the Father; as the body of Christ, which exists under the rule of the risen and ascended Lord who is its head; and as the temple of the Holy Spirit, a community of living members which Jesus Christ is building and which the Spirit of God has made into the dwelling place of the living God.

Without the Spirit, the Church ceases to be the Church. We are like living stones being 'built into a spiritual house, to be a holy priesthood, to offer spiritual sacrifices acceptable to God through Jesus Christ' (1 Peter 2:5). We are held together by the Spirit who is the 'bond of peace', the creator and sustainer of fellowship between us all (Ephesians 4:3, 16). Without the Spirit, the Church cannot do the work of God effectively. The dependence of the people of God on the Spirit of God is complete.

It is certainly not the case, therefore, that the Spirit is the exclusive possession of an élite within the Church, a group of the 'super-spiritual' who have graduated to their spiritual A levels while the rest struggle with their GCSEs: the Spirit is God's gift to the whole Church and to all believers. Neither can it be true that the Spirit is an 'optional extra', about whom the majority of good Christians need not concern themselves. The Spirit of God is absolutely essential for the very life of the whole people of God and every member of it. Without the Spirit we are not even Christians, since 'you are not in the flesh; you are in the Spirit, since the Spirit of God dwells in you. Anyone who does not have the Spirit of Christ does not belong to him' (Romans 8:9). The Spirit is as essential for the Church as is breath for the human body. Where the wind of the Spirit does not blow, there is simply an absence of spiritual life. These are strong assertions, so it is necessary to justify them from the New Testament.

THE SPIRIT AND THE GATHERING OF THE CHURCH

As we have seen, the Church came into being on the day of Pentecost, when the disciples of Jesus were together. It is recorded:

And suddenly from heaven there came a sound like the rush of a violent wind, and it filled the entire house where they were sitting. Divided tongues, as of fire, appeared among them, and a tongue rested on each of them. All of them were filled with the Holy Spirit and began to speak in other languages, as the Spirit gave them ability.
ACTS 2:2–4

Now it is certainly true that the history of the people of God can be traced further back than Pentecost. Indeed, it is with the call of Abraham that the origins of God's distinctive people may be found (Genesis 12:1–3). In addition, we see Jesus intentionally gathering a new community around himself when he appointed twelve apostles to be with him (Mark 3:13–19). The roots and the foundations of the Christian Church are therefore ancient and deep. But with the gift of the Spirit a decisive change comes about, as the new age of messianic fulfilment inaugurated by Jesus is extended across the face of the earth. In this new age, the Christian Church is centre-stage, and it is appropriate to speak of Pentecost as the beginning of the Church. At a later stage, when the Spirit also came upon the Gentiles, Cornelius and his household, the apostle Peter related his experience of this event: 'And as I began to speak, the Holy Spirit fell upon them just as it had upon us at the beginning' (Acts 11:15). For him, the coming of the Spirit at Pentecost was 'the beginning': the beginning of the new age and also of the community of the new age, the Christian Church.

Acts 2 describes this original coming of the Spirit, bringing the Church into being. As we have already seen, in it there are some significant parallels with the Old Testament, including the idea of the Spirit as wind and fire. The experience that the apostles entered into is also somewhat reminiscent of the way the Spirit came upon the 70 elders in Numbers 11:24–25:

So Moses went out and told the people the words of the Lord; and he gathered seventy elders of the people, and placed them all around the tent. Then the Lord came down in the cloud and spoke to him, and took some of the spirit that was on him and put it on the seventy elders; and when the spirit rested upon them, they prophesied. But they did not do so again.

When the Spirit came at Pentecost, the apostles were constrained to declare the deeds of God in other languages, and people from 'every nation under heaven' were able to hear the wonders of God in their own languages (Acts 2:5–12). When this passage in Acts is contrasted with the story of the tower of Babel in Genesis 11:1–9, we begin to understand the meaning of Pentecost. At the tower of Babel, the judgment of God led to the division of the people of the earth into language groups, dividing and separating them. By dividing them through language barriers, God set limits to the evil that they could do as one concerted whole. On the day of Pentecost, the precise opposite happened: instead of mutual incomprehension, 'each one heard them speaking in the native language of each' (Acts 2:6). This represents a reversal of the judgment of Babel: a reuniting of fractured and divided humanity. Because of the Spirit of God, a new people was formed, drawn from every nation under the sun and understanding a common language, that of faith in Jesus Christ as the Messiah.

The Spirit of God initiated the Church in this way. He brought it into being and is the means of its coming to birth. The Church began therefore as the community of the Spirit, and the way it began is the way it is called to continue if it is to be faithful to its origins. Without the Spirit, the Church would not and could not exist as the new, restored people of God.

THE BAPTISM OF THE HOLY SPIRIT

At this point it is helpful to take our first look at a phrase much discussed and much contested in recent years, that of 'baptism in the Holy Spirit'. Once we understand that Pentecost marks the beginning of the age of the Spirit, we are in a position to understand the prophecy of John the Baptist recorded in some form in each of the Gospels:

I baptize you with water for repentance, but one who is more powerful than I is coming after me; I am not worthy to carry his sandals. He will baptize you with the Holy Spirit and with fire. His winnowing-fork is in his hand, and he will clear his threshing-floor and will gather his wheat into the granary; but the chaff he will burn with unquenchable fire.
MATTHEW 3:11–12; COMPARE MARK 1:8; LUKE 3:16; JOHN 1:32–34

Similar words are also found on the lips of the risen Christ, with clear reference to the event of Pentecost: 'This… is what you have heard from me; for John baptized with water, but you will be baptized with the Holy Spirit not many days from now' (Acts 1:4–5).

The baptism of the Holy Spirit appears to convey the entirety of what comes to fulfilment in the new age and in the Church because of Jesus Christ. What is to happen is infinitely greater than the baptism of water and repentance practised by John. Indeed, so much greater is it to be that Jesus himself could say about John, 'Truly I tell you, among those born of women no one has arisen greater than John the Baptist; yet the least in the kingdom of heaven is greater than he' (Matthew 11:11).

This is not really a discussion about the personal greatness of John or anybody else so much as a statement about John's relationship to the new age of messianic fulfilment. John looked forward to that age and called people to prepare to enter it. But those who are living in that age, the age of the 'kingdom of heaven', are greater than he by means of the events that they have lived to see and be a part of. What is to happen through the Holy Spirit surpasses anything that has gone before. To be baptized by Christ through the Spirit into the new age is to enter into this new reality of fulfilment with all the life-changing potential that it involves. This includes the outpouring of power on the Church and its members so that they may be witnesses (Acts 1:8), but also comprises all the other aspects of the work of God in those who believe in the time of messianic fulfilment.

What we are seeking to guard against here is the downscaling of the 'baptism of the Spirit' into a personalized, individual spiritual experience, when it is so much more expansive. First we must understand the full, epoch-making reach of the baptism of the Spirit poured out by the world's Messiah. As the Church came into being through the coming of the Spirit on the day of Pentecost, so now individuals enter into the Church only when the Spirit comes to them and incorporates them into the body of Christ, causing the age of fulfilment to dawn upon them. This is the meaning of 1 Corinthians 12:12–13, where Paul says, 'For just as the body is one and has many members, and all the members of the body, though many, are one body, so it is with Christ. For in the one Spirit we were all baptized into one body—Jews or Greeks, slaves or free—and we were all made to drink of one Spirit.'

We see here how appropriate it is that the Church should mark the entry of new members to the body through the act of baptism.

Baptism is rich in symbolism. Among its meanings is that of being plunged into a new realm, the realm of the Spirit, just as a person is plunged into the waters of baptism. But this is accompanied by the idea that, in baptism, we are being buried with Christ (Romans 6:3–4). We are being joined to him in such a way as to share in the benefits he has gained for us, the benefits of having been taken down into death so that the old nature that holds us fast can be put to death, and then raised into a new life in fellowship with the risen Lord.

As it is through the Spirit that we are baptized into the body, so baptism of the Spirit, like baptism in water, needs to be understood at several levels. It is the means whereby, through the Spirit, we are joined to Christ and made to participate in his life-giving grace. It is also the means of our being empowered to live both a holy life and a spiritually effective one. The Spirit is the hallmark of the Church and of the believer within the Church, and so clarifies for us why Paul can say emphatically, 'Anyone who does not have the Spirit of Christ does not belong to him' (Romans 8:9). Without the Spirit, we have not even arrived at first base.

What this means for the individual, we shall consider more closely in the next chapter, but the life of the Christian individual always needs to be understood in the context of the Christian community. First, therefore, we consider what the baptism of the Spirit might mean for the whole Church.

THE CHURCH, THE SPIRIT AND THE AGE OF FULFILMENT

As we have now noted several times, the coming of the Spirit on the day of Pentecost was more than the outpouring of spiritual power upon the early believers. It was the beginning of a new age, the dawn of the age of fulfilment. This is the meaning of the prophecy of Joel, which was quoted by Peter in explanation of the events that people were seeing and hearing. It begins, 'In the last days it will be, God declares, that I will pour out my Spirit on all flesh' (Acts 2:17; see Joel 2:28). Peter then goes on to speak of the activity of the Spirit in God's people and connects it with the upheavals that are to take place in the world 'before the coming of the Lord's great and glorious day' (Acts 2:20). The point is that the coming of the Spirit at Pentecost is part of the eschatological (that is, end-time) fulfilment of Old Testament prophecies concerning the world's final liberation.

This day of fulfilment had already begun in the ministry of Jesus, as is frequently indicated in the Gospels (for example, Luke 1:46–55). Jesus came preaching that the time was fulfilled and that the kingdom of God had drawn near. The appropriate way to receive the kingdom was with repentance and faith (Mark 1:15). Jesus' powerful ministry of driving out the forces of evil and restoring people both to fellowship with God and to their true selves was a clear indication that the kingdom of God had come (Luke 11:20). It was for such a time as this, and for the fulfilment of this Old Testament expectation, that the Spirit of the Lord was poured out upon Jesus (Luke 3:21–22; 4:18–19). First the kingdom comes in, with Jesus of Nazareth, and then it is extended by him to those who receive and welcome him.

When Jesus was anointed with the Spirit at his baptism, it was not because he previously lacked the Holy Spirit. If John the Baptist was filled with the Spirit from before his birth (Luke 1:15), how much more must Jesus have been! Rather, when Jesus was anointed at his baptism, a new age dawned, the token of which was the coming of the Spirit in a new way. The age that dawned was that of fulfilment and liberation, of the new covenant, 'the new heart and the new spirit' which the prophets had looked forward to and which had been long delayed (Jeremiah 31:31–34; Ezekiel 18:31). At his baptism, Jesus was equipped by the Spirit to be the one through whom that age might break into the world of human beings, liberating them from the oppressions of evil and of the evil one. This is what immediately began to happen once he was propelled on his way by the empowering Spirit (see Luke 4:31–37).

Understanding this enables us to grasp what happened for the Church at the day of Pentecost. At that time, and on the basis of what Christ achieved in his ministry, his death and his resurrection, the Spirit came on the Church, bringing the age of fulfilment upon those who believe. Empowered by the Spirit, they became agents of this age of fulfilment. This brings us to a further point.

THE CHURCH OF THE END-TIME

The Church is the community of people who have already entered into the age of fulfilment. In other words, while continuing to be a part of the created order, outwardly indistinguishable from the rest of humankind, they have already entered into a dimension of God's life which means that the power of the transcendent God is transforming them. This is what Hebrews 6:4–5 means when it refers to those who 'have once been enlightened, and have tasted the heavenly gift, and have shared in the Holy Spirit, and have tasted the goodness of the word of God and the powers of the age to come'. Similarly, Paul can refer to Christians as those 'on whom the ends of the ages have come' (1 Corinthians 10:11) and to the Holy Spirit as a present 'pledge of our inheritance towards redemption as God's own people, to the praise of his glory' (Ephesians 1:14).

Each of these texts suggests that the future is already present in the Church. The coming of the kingdom of God refers to the entry of a power and a presence into the present, which comes from the future that God has planned and towards which we are moving. By the Spirit, the power of the age to come is present and manifest in the Church.

This must count as another of the differences between the activity of the Spirit in the Old Testament and that in the New. Through the Spirit, the Church of the new covenant is experiencing a foretaste of the future kingdom, experiencing in part the glory and power of a world that is wholly at peace with God and with itself. Of course, this experience is only partial and imperfect, but enough of God's future is glimpsed in the worship and fellowship of the Church to give strength and hope for the arduous journey that still awaits those who travel there. Contrasting the blessings of the new age with what was known of the old, the author of Hebrews proclaimed:

But you have come to Mount Zion and to the city of the living God, the heavenly Jerusalem, and to innumerable angels in festal gathering, and to the assembly of the firstborn who are enrolled in heaven, and to God the judge of all, and to the spirits of the righteous made perfect, and to Jesus, the mediator of a new covenant, and to the sprinkled blood that speaks a better word than the blood of Abel.

HEBREWS 12:22–24

Most of what the writer describes here is eschatological in nature, to be fully realized only with the consummation of the ages. But these realities are ones to which believers in Jesus have already come. They already form the substance of what we have entered into in Christ. This is indeed the age of the Spirit. The Church is indeed the community of the future.

THE CHURCH IN THE POWER OF THE SPIRIT

The coming of the Spirit on the Church was a powerful and mighty act of God. The Spirit of fellowship came to create a dynamic and transforming communion with God and with others in Christ. This is precisely what we see in the early chapters of Acts, as individuals carried along by the Spirit repented, believed, were baptized and received the Holy Spirit (2:38). A new community came into being, where a greater bond surpassed and made relative the old ties of culture, class, possessions and self-interest (2:42–47).

In these descriptions, Luke is being more than a careful historian, although we must certainly credit him with that concern (Luke 2:1–4). He is describing the Church as an exemplary community. What the Church was in its origins is the clue to what it should continue to be. Behind Luke's historical concern there is also a theological one: the Church is at its best when it is the kind of community described in these early pages of its history. In all this the Church is, in the here and now, the expression of the age to come. It lives by the power of the Spirit as surely as it came to be by the Spirit.

In community terms, this may be seen in the following evidences of the Spirit's life.

- The Church worships by the Spirit.
- The Church serves by the Spirit.
- The Church fulfils its mission by the Spirit.
- The Church is guided by the Spirit.

The Church worships by the Spirit

When the Spirit came, in the early chapters of Acts, one sign of his coming was that the worship of God came readily to the people of God. In Acts 2:4, they are filled with the Spirit of God and begin to speak in other tongues. In 2:11, this is interpreted to mean that they are 'declaring the wonders of God' (NIV). In 2:42–47 they are said to be 'filled with awe' (NIV) and to meet together every day in the temple courts, praising God. When the Spirit falls upon the household of Cornelius, they too speak in tongues and praise God (10:46). There is an inescapable link here between the Spirit and worship. Those who are filled with the Holy Spirit cannot help but give expression to it in praise.

Paul identifies one of the distinguishing marks of Christians in the fact that they 'worship in the Spirit of God and boast in Christ Jesus and have no confidence in the flesh' (Philippians 3:3). The Spirit himself enables the Church to know and confess 'Abba, Father' in worship (Romans 8:15), and as the Church does so it shows that it has been united by the Spirit with Christ, sharing in the Son's relationship with the Father. Jesus himself worshipped the Father by the Spirit (Luke 10:21) and taught his disciples to pray, saying, 'Our Father in heaven' (Matthew 6:9). He also defined true worship as worship in 'spirit and truth' (John 4:24). This is a con-trast with the kind of worship that is primarily outward observance rather than heartfelt intimacy with God. It also indicates, however, that since to worship the Father is to have living access to him through the Son, this can be our experience only in so far as the Spirit draws us into the life of God and enables us to respond to God in praise and thanks.

It is clear from the list of spiritual gifts in 1 Corinthians 12:7–11 that gatherings for worship were marked by the manifestation of the Spirit for the common good. Far from being dominated by one person, or taking the form of ritualized repetition, early Christian worship meetings were times of participation, when people with varying gifts could pray or speak for the good of all (1 Corinthians 14:26–33). They were dynamic and free community events, and it was the Spirit who inspired and enabled the participation. This was not unstructured worship (although, as Paul indicated, it needed to be carried through in an orderly fashion), but worship led by the Spirit.

The Church serves by the Spirit

The place of service is seen in the emphasis on spiritual gifts, the 'charismata' or 'gifts of grace', which have been bestowed on the Church and its members by the Spirit. There are at least three lists of spiritual gifts given in the New Testament, and none of them is identical.

- In Romans 12:6–8, the list includes prophesying, serving, teaching, encouraging, contributing and leading, all necessary gifts in the community life of the Church.

- In Ephesians 4:7–13, the gifts of Christ are seen as people who exercise leadership functions within the Church: apostles, prophets, evangelists, pastors and teachers (or, as some people insist, pastor-teachers).
- In 1 Corinthians 12:7–11, the gifts listed include the word of wisdom, the word of knowledge, faith, gifts of healing, miraculous powers, prophecy, discernment of spirits, speaking in tongues and interpretation of tongues. These appear from the context to be gifts that might have found expression particularly in early Christian gatherings.

It may be helpful to make a number of points about these gifts. First, the lists cited appear to be *representative samples* of spiritual gifts rather than an exhaustive tally. No doubt there are as many other gifts as the Spirit determines there should be. Certainly the custom in some circles of referring to 'the nine gifts' (those in 1 Corinthians 12), as if this were the sum total of possibilities, seems unnecessarily restrictive. It is perhaps more accurate to think in terms of the multi-faceted work of the Holy Spirit, which can take many forms and find expression in varying spiritual gifts. When the New Testament specifies individual gifts, it is referring to those that were known about or at issue in the particular contexts under discussion.

Second, it is *unhelpful to make too rigid definitions* of individual spiritual gifts. No doubt there is considerable overlap between, for instance, a word of knowledge (a revelation of an item of information) and a word of wisdom (a revelation of a wise course of action). Perhaps, also, the boundary between exhortation and prophecy is not very clear: much of what is called prophecy today may better be understood as exhortation. It must be acknowledged that the precise character of some of these gifts cannot be deduced from the contexts in which they are mentioned. The tendency has been, therefore, to interpret them in the light of contemporary Pentecostal or charismatic experience, and this runs the danger of reading back these experiences into the text. It may be that the practice yields accurate conclusions, but integrity in handling scripture should lead us to be cautious in our approach and modest in our claims.

Third, it is helpful to understand *the spectrum of spiritual gifts*. The gifts already mentioned include:

* experiences that are highly intuitive (such as speaking in tongues or prophecy).
* abilities that are largely rational (such as teaching or leading).
* qualities that are partly circumstantial (such as contributing: some people just have more money than others).

What Paul is really trying to stress is that, whatever form the activity of the Spirit takes, it is a gift and not something to boast about. It would be a mistake to imagine that any one gift is better than another because it is, say, more intuitive and therefore apparently more 'mystical'. Likewise, it would be wrong to devalue a gift because it is less rational than others, which is possibly why Paul warns, 'Do not quench the Spirit. Do not despise the words of prophets' (1 Thessalonians 5:19–20).

All gifts have their place in the service of the Church and of God. Because the Spirit is Lord of all aspects of our nature, whether of our conscious intuition or our circumstances, we should expect him to work through all parts of our lives. What determines whether a gift is really spiritual is not its unusual character or the drama with which it is employed but the purpose for which it is used and the effect it has in building up the Church. This is Paul's whole argument in 1 Corinthians 12, a chapter that will repay careful study on this topic. The Spirit manifests himself through the members of Christ's body for the common good of all, not for the private gratification of some (1 Corinthians 12:7, 24–26). The spiritual value of a gift is to be measured according to whether it 'edifies' or 'builds up' God's people (1 Corinthians 14:1–5).

Finally, our *model for understanding* spiritual gifts is important.

Often they have been thought of rather statically as individual gifts that individuals possess in a rather proprietorial way. We are then tempted to compare ourselves with others and either feel proud or inferior, as the case may be, depending on how many and what kind of gifts we imagine ourselves to possess. This tendency to compare oneself with others was clearly already going on in the New Testament Church (1 Corinthians 12:21–25), and has certainly shown itself from time to time in charismatic circles. Yet spiritual pride is one of the most distasteful of all the sins, since it takes what we have been given by God out of sheer generosity and grace and turns it into an occasion for sinful boasting.

A better way of thinking might be to recognize that, strictly speaking, we do not 'possess' any gift of God, as though it were somehow resident in ourselves. We are, however, indwelt by the Spirit, and the Spirit is able freely to manifest any gift through any Christian, according to the need of the situation. This is sometimes called the 'situational' view of the gifts in contrast to the 'constituted' view. It stresses that in any given situation we may be given the gift that is needed for the moment. It is not as though Christians carry around with themselves the gift of healing or prophecy to be applied at any moment they choose; rather, God gives from moment to moment what is needed. This offers a more dynamic, and a more modest, way of thinking of the Spirit and God's gifts, and stresses that our steadfast relationship to the Spirit of God is the crucial factor in our service of God. Far from being divided into the gifted and the ungifted, Christians share a radical equality. They have nothing to bring to God other than their humble availability to his work. None of us has anything that we did not receive from God in the first place.

THE CHURCH FULFILS ITS MISSION BY THE SPIRIT

The Spirit is said by Jesus to be sent to us from the Father and to come from the Father (John 15:26). We might describe him as the outgoing Spirit. Wherever the Spirit goes, there is a corresponding outgoing movement. When the Spirit came upon the early Church, the immediate response was an outgoing one. The apostles spoke the work of God boldly and effectively, with the result that thousands were converted to Christ and joined the Church. We see the pattern repeated in Acts 4: the Spirit came upon the Church again so that 'they were all filled with the Holy Spirit and spoke the word of God with boldness' (v. 31). From that base the Christian faith has continued to expand to the ends of the earth, and the book of Acts records the rapid growth of the early Church in the power of the Spirit.

Church history repeats the lesson that people find life in God when the Spirit revives the Church and thrusts it into proclamation and service in the communities in which it is set. The Spirit empowers the Church for mission—joining in the outgoing movement of God into the world, seeking that people should be reconciled to God and so changing lives and transforming communities.

THE CHURCH IS GUIDED BY THE SPIRIT

In fulfilling its mission to the world, the Church of Christ (and individual churches within the whole Church) needs the guidance of the Spirit. The difficulties and challenges that the Church faces are many and various and change from context to context. There are decisions to be made about how to serve the cause of Christ in the very different circumstances and cultures within which it is set. The Bible contains the fundamental truths of the faith, but it does not legislate for any and every circumstance or decision that we must make, or for how those truths are to be applied in each situation.

At this point we are relying on the wisdom that comes from continual reflection on God's word and our ability to sense the mind of the Spirit. Because we are all fallible, discerning the mind of the Spirit on many issues is best done by the Church as a community. For this reason, Jesus told his disciples that they would not be left in the dark once he had left them: 'When the Spirit of truth comes, he will guide you into all the truth; for he will not speak on his own, but will speak whatever he hears, and he will declare to you the things that are to come' (John 16:13).

We see this promise being fulfilled in Acts:

- In 11:28 we find the prophet Agabus predicting through the Spirit a severe famine, enabling the church to take action.
- In 13:2 the church at Antioch is directed by the Spirit to set aside Barnabas and Saul for mission work.
- In 15:28 the church is guided by the Spirit over a highly divisive issue at the council of Jerusalem and is able to say at the end of its consultations, 'For it has seemed good to the Holy Spirit and to us…'.
- In 16:6 we hear of Paul 'having been forbidden by the Holy Spirit to speak the word in Asia'. The following verse indicates that when they tried to enter Bithynia 'the Spirit of Jesus did not allow them'.
- In 20:22–23 Paul says, 'As a captive to the Spirit, I am on my way to Jerusalem, not knowing what will happen to me there, except that the Holy Spirit testifies to me in every city that imprisonment and persecutions are waiting for me.'

The church exists under the Lordship of Christ in the Spirit and therefore is assured of the guiding presence of the Spirit in its mission.

SUMMARY

We have noted in this chapter that the Church in the New Testament is the community of the Holy Spirit. It has its origin and its life in the Spirit of God. Where this ceases to be the case, the

Church no longer exists in its true form but has become a society of religious people. So this chapter has direct relevance to the way the Church is now. The task of recovering the sense of being a dynamic community, guided by God, which lives, works, worships, proclaims and serves in the power of the Spirit, is a crucial challenge for the Church in every place and generation.

——— Chapter 7 ———

THE SPIRIT AND THE BELIEVER

The ground we have covered so far enables us to approach the subject of the Spirit and the individual believer. Often, when we think about the Spirit, the individual's experience immediately comes to mind. This book has sought to avoid that emphasis by looking first to the wider works of the Spirit in creation and redemption, and then examining the Spirit's work in the Christian community. In doing this, we have guarded against reducing the Spirit to a concern with our own experience and feelings.

Yet it is entirely true that the Spirit is the one through whom God lays hold of us and comes to us as individuals. Christian faith is not a private affair but it is most certainly a personal one. Now we are in a position to see, in the light of all that has been said, what the Spirit does in individual believers. If we may rightly speak of the Spirit as God on the inside of God, we may also speak of the Spirit as God on the inside of our own lives—God at his closest to us.

In Chapter 4 we considered the work of the Spirit as the giver of Jesus and traced the ways in which the humanity of Jesus was the result of the Spirit's activity. In the Church, which comes together in Jesus' name, the Spirit is concerned to produce a community of people made in the image of Christ. In the individual members of that community, God's Spirit is concerned through Jesus to produce people who are like Christ. Romans 8:29 states, 'For those whom (God) foreknew he also predestined to be conformed to the image of his Son, in order that he might be the firstborn within a large family.'

The role of the Spirit in this work of transformation is expressed clearly in 2 Corinthians 3:17–18, verses we have referred to several times, which read:

Now the Lord is the Spirit, and where the Spirit of the Lord is, there is freedom. And all of us, with unveiled faces, seeing the glory of the Lord as though reflected in a mirror, are being transformed into the same image from one degree of glory to another; for this comes from the Lord, the Spirit.

It is the Spirit's work to do in us what has already been done in Christ, but it is through Christ that this work is to be done. Christ has pioneered the way. To use a commercial and marketing analogy, Christ is the prototype of a new humanity, the one in whom truly God-centred humanity has been worked out. The Church is the pilot project, the community in which the prototype is being reproduced in large numbers, and the world is the market that is to be reached with this new way of being human. Christ has opened up a new relationship with God and has fulfilled and completed humanity. He is the true human being. The Spirit's work is now to take what has been done in Jesus and reproduce it in those who believe, by enabling us conform to Christ's image. We shall see, therefore, that in describing the Spirit's work in the believer, there are some direct parallels with the description in Chapter 4 of the Spirit's work in Christ.

THE SPIRIT'S PREPARATORY WORK

As the Spirit prepared the way for the coming of Christ into the world, so the Spirit prepares the way for us to come to the Father through Christ. In doing this, the Spirit must awaken us to our sense of need and inspire us to place our truth in Christ and his saving work.

The Spirit convicts us of our need

The Spirit of fellowship is about the task of restoring our broken relationship with the Father. The first step in this process is to make us aware that we are lost and need to be reconciled to God. The human condition is described in scripture in stark terms. As far as Jesus is concerned, we are lost, in the wrong place and heading in the wrong direction (Luke 15; 19:10). Paul puts it like this:

You were dead through the trespasses and sins in which you once lived, following the course of this world, following the ruler of the power of the air, the spirit that is now at work among those who are disobedient. All of us once lived among them in the passions of our flesh, following the desires of flesh and senses, and we were by nature children of wrath, like everyone else.

EPHESIANS 2:1–3

This is not to say that human beings are demons and that nothing good can be said about them. It means that, as far as God was concerned, before we were made alive in Christ we were insensitive towards God and enclosed in ourselves, going along with the rest and unaware of the extent to which we were simply conforming to the crowd, prisoners to the prevailing culture. Out of this condition we needed to be awakened. Jesus indicated that on the coming of the Spirit, 'he will prove the world wrong about sin and righteousness and judgment: about sin, because they do not believe in me; about righteousness, because I am going to the Father and you will see me no longer; about judgment, because the ruler of this world has been condemned' (John 16:8–11).

Paraphrased, this means that the Spirit will show that people are sinners because of their unbelief in Christ, that Jesus is righteous and has been exalted, and that the ruler of this world has been judged at the cross. The Spirit's work is to convince people of the truth of these things and bring them to awareness of their need. This is what we see happening at Pentecost: 'Now when [the people] heard this, they were cut to the heart and said to Peter and to the other apostles, "Brothers, what should we do?"' (Acts 2:37). Likewise, Paul says of the Thessalonians, 'Our message of the gospel came to you not in word only, but also in power and in the Holy Spirit and with full conviction' (1 Thessalonians 1:5).

The Spirit enlightens our minds

To be 'dead through trespasses and sins' means to be unable to help ourselves. It means that someone has to help us climb out of the pit in which we find ourselves. We must make our way to God, but we can do it only in response to an influence upon our lives that comes from outside ourselves, which both prepares us and liberates us to make our response to God in repentance (a change of mind) and faith. This is the work of the Holy Spirit in opening up our wills and affections to the love and grace of God. It is impossible for anyone to come to Christ unless drawn by the Father (John 6:44). This involves a kind of enlightenment, by means of which eyes are opened and darkened minds are enabled to understand. The Spirit of God is at work in the world doing just this, drawing people to Christ, enlightening them (Ephesians 1:17–18) and opening minds to the truth that is in Jesus (1 Corinthians 2:8–10, 14–16). The Spirit who prepared the world to receive Christ in his incarnation is at work in us, preparing the way for the Son of God to come and make his home within us.

THE SPIRIT'S REGENERATING WORK

The preparatory work of the Spirit has as its goal the regeneration, or new birth, of the individual. This is referred to in John 3:3–8, where Jesus teaches that a person can neither see nor enter the kingdom of God unless born of the Spirit: 'Very truly, I tell you, no one can enter the kingdom of God without being born of water and Spirit. What is born of the flesh is flesh, and what is born of the Spirit is spirit' (vv. 5–6).

To be 'born of water' might in this context mean physical birth, preceded as it is by the breaking of the sac of water in which a baby is held. In this case, Jesus would be saying that the physical birth of individuals, bringing them into normal human life, must be paralleled by a spiritual birth which is not humanly produced but is the work of the Spirit. This work makes us spiritually alive, as though we had been born spiritually, and brings us under the saving rule of God. It issues in trust in Jesus Christ, which opens the door into eternal life (John 3:16). Equally, the word 'water' could be a reference to the kind of baptism practised by John the Baptist, a baptism of repentance. To be born of water and Spirit, therefore, is to come to a new life through repentance and by the enlivening work of the Spirit of God in the heart.

In particular, we should notice here that just as the Spirit was the means whereby Jesus was conceived in the womb of Mary, so the same Spirit who brought Jesus to be alive in her is the author of spiritual birth in our own hearts. As Jesus was born of the Spirit, so are we.

The mystery of how it happens

When someone is born 'from above' or 'of the Spirit' (John 3:3, 5), there is a sense of mystery, just as there is when a baby is born. In their own ways, both of these events are miracles. To think that, within nine months, a child can be conceived and develop into an amazingly complex individual, possessed of its own personality, is astonishing. So it is with new birth. There is a sense of mystery and wonder about the way a person becomes aware of needing God and then turns to him. We cannot fully explain it but are grateful that it happens. We do not know why this particular person should come into new life in this way and at this time but we witness it happening. This sense of wonder and of the sovereign freedom of God is what Jesus means when he refers to the Spirit as the wind: 'The wind blows where it chooses, and you hear the sound of it, but you do not know where it comes from or where it goes. So it is with everyone who is born of the Spirit' (John 3:8).

The result of this activity is that lives are inwardly changed so that those who experience it receive a 'new spirit and a new heart' (Ezekiel 18:31; 36:26). Regeneration, the new birth, is an inward change brought about by God in the hidden depths of the human personality. In another place it is described in this way:

But when the goodness and loving-kindness of God our Saviour appeared, he saved us, not because of any works of righteousness that we had done, but according to his mercy, through the water of rebirth and renewal of the Holy Spirit. This Spirit he poured out on us richly through Jesus Christ our Saviour, so that, having been justified by his grace, we might become heirs according to the hope of eternal life.
TITUS 3:4–7

The word by which it happens

How all this comes to pass is a mystery to us, but it is clear that the Holy Spirit operates through the speaking of the gospel. So in Galatians 3:2 Paul says, 'Did you receive the Spirit by doing the law or by believing what you heard?'

The power and importance of the word that is preached is implied everywhere in the Bible, but in Ephesians 6:17 it is clearly expressed: 'Take the helmet of salvation, and the sword of the Spirit, which is the word of God.' True, accurate and gracious speaking of the gospel is the sharp edge by which the Spirit penetrates into people's lives. The close connection of word and Spirit should not surprise us. We have seen that words need breath (spirit) in order to be uttered, that the life-bringing word was spoken into creation by the Spirit in the beginning, and that the human life of Jesus, the Word of God, came to utterance, as it were, through the Spirit. So it continues to be. The spoken word of the gospel receives its power and force through the Holy Spirit who is active in bringing people to new birth.

THE SPIRIT'S ADOPTING WORK

When a baby is born, he or she is the child of the parents. When believers are born of the Spirit, they become children of God. This means more than just that they are forgiven. Forgiveness and the remission of sins are certainly part of God's gracious dealings with us, but it is possible to be forgiven by someone and still not be a member of their family. Yet the love of God is such that when we receive his forgiveness he also makes us members of his family.

Expressed theologically, adoption is more than justification. Justification is the work of God whereby God remits our sins and accepts us into relationship. Adoption is the work of God that brings us into the most intimate form of communion with God as his beloved and favoured children. Clearly we do not share the eternal sonship that Jesus the Son does, but we can be brought into the family of God. It is the Holy Spirit who adopts us into God's family and brings us into this personal family union with the Father. Romans 8:15–17 makes this clear:

For you did not receive a spirit of slavery to fall back into fear, but you have received a spirit of adoption. When we cry, 'Abba! Father!' it is that very Spirit bearing witness with our spirit that we are children of God... and joint heirs with Christ—if, in fact, we suffer with him so that we may also be glorified with him.

In Galatians 4:6–7 similar words occur: 'And because you are children, God has sent the Spirit of his Son into our hearts, crying, "Abba! Father!" So you are no longer a slave but a child, and if a child then also an heir, through God.'

Adopted into a new relationship

These verses from scripture are of the greatest importance. They show to us once more the intimate connection between the work of the Son and that of the Spirit. The Spirit is not at work independently of the Son but is drawing us through the Son into the relationship that the Son shares with the Father. What the believer receives through the Spirit is nothing less than living participation in the relationship between the Son and the Father by means of the Spirit. This is truly to participate in God.

Jesus' life was marked by the intimacy of the relationship he knew with God. He called God 'Father' (Luke 10:21). Much has been made of the word 'Abba', which in Aramaic was the intimate family word for the father of the family. Sometimes it is said that the equivalent English word is 'Daddy', but this is misleading since many English-speaking children grow out of using the word 'Daddy' at a certain point and feel awkward about using it thereafter. Consequently, when preachers confidently assert that this is what 'Abba' means, they may be in danger, at least in the ears of some people, of trivializing the word. The word 'Abba' could be used between children and their father for a whole lifetime and carries no connotation of childishness.

Becoming a child of God is made possible through the atoning life, death and resurrection of the Son. He came down and participated fully and completely in our life and our fate so that through him we might be lifted into his relationship to the Father. What was made possible through the Son in his redeeming work among us is made actual by the Spirit, who relates us to the Father through the Son. We become God's children by sharing with the Son a living relationship to the Father, an access to his presence that heals and restores our broken lives:

But now in Christ Jesus you who once were far off have been brought near by the blood of Christ. For he is our peace... So he came and proclaimed peace to you who were far off and peace to those who were near; for through him both of us [in other words, Jews and Gentiles] have access in one Spirit to the Father.
EPHESIANS 2:13–14, 17–18

103

Adopted to share in the communion of God

Once more, we see here the work of the Spirit of fellowship. The one who is the eternal bond of fellowship between Father and Son is the same one who creates fellowship for human beings through the Son with the Father. 2 Peter 1:3–4 expresses it in this way:

His divine power has given us everything needed for life and godliness, through the knowledge of him who called us by his own glory and goodness. Thus he has given us, through these things, his precious and very great promises, so that through them you may escape from the corruption that is in the world because of lust, and may become participants in the divine nature.

We share in God as his children by the Spirit through the Son. A more amazing thought is difficult to imagine! We are quickly led on to further thoughts.

THE SPIRIT'S ASSURING WORK

If God adopts us by this Spirit, it is that same Spirit who inwardly assures us that we are indeed children of God.

The 'heart strangely warmed'

It would be presumptuous of us to claim this relationship were it not that the Spirit grants a deep, inward conviction that it is so. The Spirit creates a spontaneous awareness that God is our 'Abba' or Father, and this is the language and the experience of worship (Romans 8:15); the Spirit also produces in us the deeply felt and intuitive recognition that we now know God in this way: 'It is that very Spirit bearing witness with our spirit that we are God's children' (Romans 8:16). These words speak of the Christian believer's experience of knowing profoundly and persuasively that he or she belongs to God.

This is what the founder of Methodism, John Wesley, meant when he spoke of his heart being 'strangely warmed'. For Wesley, this was the moment of his conversion, the time when he turned to God in a decisive way. We might suspect that it was rather the moment when, having turned to God previously, he received the assurance of his acceptance and sonship. At any rate, it was a supremely significant moment for him and for the movement that he founded, for which 'experimental (or experiential) religion' and 'proving God' (that is, as a reality in one's own experience) were dynamic elements. The experience of assurance defies explanation and must be understood as an awareness of the fellowship with God into which the Christian is brought, through the Spirit.

An antidote to doubt

Every Christian will know the assuring work of the Spirit but all of us also know that there are times when God seems more absent than present—times of spiritual dryness. These too have their place, since they teach us not to rely on feelings, which can be variable and unreliable, but to live in faith and trust. Yet to recognize that the Spirit brings assurance may help us to understand many experiences that are commonplace in the Church. Most of us need to experience some form of renewal at some time or other because our awareness of God wanes. Church history is full of renewal movements that have sought to bring to the wider Church a new sense of God's presence and power. It is helpful to understand that, often, these are new manifestations of the assuring work of the Spirit breaking out among God's people.

This explains why believers often testify to coming to a new place in their walk with God. Different terms have been used at different times. Sometimes people speak of being 'baptized in the Spirit' or 'sanctified'. Sometimes the renewal experience is accompanied by receiving a spiritual gift, such as speaking in tongues. Rather than engaging in extended debates about which of these terms are correct and which are not, it is perhaps more helpful to see all these experiences as moments when the assurance of the Holy Spirit that we are truly in Christ and truly God's children is intensified and increased within us.

There is much to give thanks for in this and absolutely nothing of which to boast. The tragedy of such movements is that they always have the potential to become divisive. Those who have entered into new experiences might regard themselves as 'those who have it', looking down on those who have not entered in as 'those who lack it'. Equally, those who are outside the new experience take offence because they feel that they are being looked down on and lack the security in God to rejoice on behalf of others. Both tendencies are symptoms of immaturity: why should any of us be threatened by the fact that others experience the assuring work of the Spirit? And why should assurance of a grace that is free and undeserved lead any of us to think more highly of ourselves than we ought?

The assurance Jesus knew

It is humbling to note that Jesus himself knew, and needed to know, moments of deep assurance. As 'one who in every respect has been tested as we are' (Hebrews 4:15), he knew times of doubt and needed the assurance of the Spirit. It is possible to see the baptism of Jesus in this light:

And when Jesus had been baptized, just as he came up from the water, suddenly the heavens were opened to him and he saw the Spirit of God descending like a dove and alighting on him. And a voice from heaven said, 'This is my Son, the Beloved, with whom I am well pleased.'
MATTHEW 3:16–17

Similarly, in Luke 10:21–22 we read, 'At that same hour, Jesus rejoiced in the Holy Spirit and said, "I thank you, Father, Lord of heaven and earth… and no one knows who the Son is except the Father, or who the Father is except the Son and anyone to whom the Son chooses to reveal him."'

Not only did Jesus know the assuring work of the Spirit by whom his relationship with the Father was sustained, but he also sets the pattern for those who belong to him and receive the same Spirit that was upon him.

THE SPIRIT'S SANCTIFYING WORK

It is sometimes said that the crisis of the new birth needs to be followed by the process of being made holy. This is what is meant by 'sanctification'. In the new birth, a person's life is radically changed from within to enable him or her to break with old, sinful patterns of living and to live a new, holy life in the power of God. The Spirit who initiated the new life is the one who sustains it—the *Holy* Spirit, or the Spirit of holiness (Romans 1:4).

Defying the downward drag

In seeking to live the Christian life, we can see similarities with an aeroplane flying. A plane has to overcome the downward drag of gravity and needs a boost in order to rise above it. Once it is flying, the laws of aerodynamics come into play to counteract the law of gravity. Similarly, as Christians, we all have to contend with the downward pull of our sinful desires and tendencies, and we are never free of this struggle. In the Spirit it is possible to rise above them, but only in so far and for as long as we are sustained by the Spirit. Without the Spirit's help, we plunge to the ground, as it were, in catastrophe. It is the Spirit who restrains the unholy tendencies with which we all struggle, keeping them in check by means of our willing submission and co-operation:

For the law of the Spirit of life in Christ Jesus has set you free from the law of sin and of death... For those who live according to the flesh set their minds on the things of the flesh, but those who live according to the Spirit set their minds on the things of the Spirit. To set the mind on the flesh is death, but to set the mind on the Spirit is life and peace... But you are not in the flesh; you are in the Spirit, since the Spirit of God dwells in you. Anyone who does not have the Spirit of Christ does not belong to him.
ROMANS 8:2, 5–6, 9

The Spirit, who is present in the life of every believing person, is the active and powerful influence of God holding at bay our sinful tendencies. The downward drag of our sinful tendencies is overcome only as we live in the power of the Spirit of God, the 'law of the Spirit of life', which sets us free from the 'law of sin and of death'.

Power for the good life

The Spirit not only restrains the evil that is in us but also releases into us the power, the divine impetus and energy, to do what is good:

Live by the Spirit, I say, and do not gratify the desires of the flesh. For what the flesh desires is opposed to the Spirit, and what the Spirit desires is opposed to the flesh... By contrast, the fruit of the Spirit is love, joy, peace, patience, kindness, generosity, faithfulness, gentleness and self-control. There is no law against such things.
GALATIANS 5:16–17, 22–23

The term 'fruit of the Spirit' helps us to see that the virtues listed are the result, or the harvest, of the Spirit's presence in our lives. God's Spirit causes them to grow and to spring forth from within us. If we wished to summarize these virtues, we could simply say that they amount to being like Christ, in whom we see these qualities held together in perfect harmony. The Spirit renews us into the image of Jesus Christ so that we are progressively changed into his likeness (2 Corinthians 3:18).

We might conveniently divide the fruit of the Spirit into inner and outer qualities. Some of the fruit that Paul lists are part of the inner experience of joy and peace. The Spirit creates a disposition within the Christian which replaces the common experiences of dejection and unrest with the joy and peace that come from knowing that, through our fellowship with God, all is well. It would be true to say that no Christian experiences these emotions all the time; nor should they. But all Christians will find themselves, at least occasionally, being surprised by deep feelings of joy or peace, and most have a sense of underlying security in God despite their outer circumstances. All this comes from the Spirit who upholds and undergirds our lives.

The inner dispositions find outward expression in the other qualities that Paul mentions, of which the first listed is of course love—the attitude that actively seeks the good of others. In a sense, the qualities that follow are simply commentaries on what the loving life looks like. The loving life is patient and kind towards others, desires and seeks only that which is good, is generous, reliable and dependable and is not subject to unpredictable moods or likely to fly off the handle. This is what we see in Jesus and this is what the Spirit is doing in us. Indeed, such qualities are the only infallible signs of the presence of the Spirit.

Paul makes it abundantly clear that although the Christian may experience all manner of remarkable things, and may manifest gifts beyond that which is normal, the only absolutely certain sign of the Spirit of God is the Christ-like love that is reproduced by him in our lives. This is particularly the point in 1 Corinthians 13, where Paul is helping believers to see that although God may well be at work in dramatic and miraculous events, not everything that is dramatic and marvellous is necessarily of God. Therefore we should not be easily or overly impressed by phenomena that pass as signs of the 'supernatural'. Rather, we are to look for love as the sign of God's true presence: 'Little children, let us love, not in word or speech, but in truth and action' (1 John 3:18).

It is also noteworthy that in Galatians 5:22 Paul refers to the 'fruit' (singular) of the Spirit, not the 'fruits' (plural). In other words, the virtues that he lists are not various options, one or other of which may be found in the Spirit-controlled life. They are the fruit of the Spirit, qualities that are all bound together in harmony and unity in the life that is truly given over to God.

Inevitably, when we read this we end up asking what is wrong with us! None of us matches up to the description that Paul gives. But if the Spirit is within us, all of us are on the road towards being made more completely like Christ. This capacity to be and do good is not humanly generated. It is a gift from God. It comes about when we live in dependence on the Spirit of God. Just as the Spirit is the breath of God that upholds creation and enables it to continue in existence, so it is the Spirit who upholds Christians and enables them to live in and for God.

Enabling sacrificial living

This godly and gracious way of living is a million miles away from the form of legalism that sees the good life as a series of rules to be obeyed. Laws and rules are necessary as ways of spelling out in specifics what a good and kind life might look like, but they do not themselves provide the power to do what is specified. This power comes from an inner change of motivation and will. The Christian life means living for God because something has happened that makes us want to do so. It is the fulfilment of the influential Old Testament prophecy, 'I will put my law within them, and I will write it on their hearts; and I will be their God, and they shall be my people' (Jeremiah 31:33).

It is the Holy Spirit, God on the inside, who writes God's holy will upon the hearts of those who believe and causes them to will that which is right. This includes enabling believers to live sacrificially. In considering the Spirit's work in Christ, we noted that 'through the eternal Spirit [he] offered himself without blemish to God' (Hebrews 9:14). The self-offering of Jesus was motivated by the Spirit, and Christians likewise are enabled to give themselves to God and for others in sacrificial service because of the Spirit within them. There are aspects of the self-offering of Christ that we are unable to imitate, since he alone could give himself in atonement as our great high priest, but in the life of service we are able to follow Jesus in his way to the cross and to present our bodies to God 'as a living sacrifice, holy and acceptable to God, which is your spiritual worship' (Romans 12:1).

THE SPIRIT'S EMPOWERING WORK

The Holy Spirit is for ever associated with the powerful events of the day of Pentecost and with the words of Jesus: 'But you will receive power when the Holy Spirit has come upon you; and you will be my witnesses in Jerusalem, in all Judea and Samaria, and to the ends of the earth' (Acts 1:8). This promise of power for witness comes in intimate relation with the preceding words: 'For John baptized with water, but you will be baptized with the Holy Spirit not many days from now' (v. 5).

As we previously noted, the term 'baptize with the Holy Spirit' raises an issue that has figured large in recent debate. The charismatic movement has insisted on the need to be 'baptized with the Spirit'—that is, to have an empowering experience of the same order as that of the disciples at Pentecost. We have already examined this subject in a preliminary way. The issues are really quite complex, but it might help to set out three options for defining 'the baptism of the Spirit'.

Empowering and equipping: Charismatic Christians have often (but by no means always) argued that baptism in the Spirit is the part of the Spirit's work that has to do with empowering and equip-ping for mission and service. Every Christian needs to be endued with power, and this should be seen as a definite experience and not just something that all Christians theoretically possess. The danger has been in dividing up Christians into two classes: those baptized in the Spirit and those not. Other Christians have rightly found this latter implication difficult to accept. Charismatics have tended to appeal to the patterns of Christian experience in Acts to justify their position.

Regeneration: The second option has been to insist that baptism in the Spirit is not primarily an empowering work but a work of regeneration. It is not to be seen as a second experience subsequent to conversion: it is conversion. Every Christian is regenerated by the Spirit and baptized into Christ, and so there cannot be two classes of Christians. Baptism in the Spirit is what happens when we are brought into the realm of the Spirit when we first repent and believe.

Those who take this position appeal to Paul, particularly to 1 Corinthians 12:13, which announces, 'For in the one Spirit we were all baptized into one body—Jews or Greeks, slaves or free—and we were all made to drink of one Spirit.' To insist, then, that people need to be baptized in the Spirit when they already have been seems disrespectful—almost like saying that someone who is a Christian needs to become a Christian. This position makes it clear that all Christians belong to the same 'class' and are not to be divided up. It obscures the fact that they do need to be empowered, however, and that exactly this is happening, among other things, on the day of Pentecost. The fact of the matter is that if all Christians have been baptized with the Spirit, many of them appear not to have noticed or to be aware of the fact.

The Christian does not become complete at conversion. To say, 'There is nothing else I need' is a perilously dangerous spiritual position to take. To safeguard against this, some prefer to avoid the language of baptism altogether and to speak of 'being filled with the Spirit', as Paul does in Ephesians 5:18. All Christians may be baptized in the Spirit, but not all are filled with the Spirit. The promise of Jesus in Acts 1:5–9 (which we see fulfilled in Acts 2) seems to indicate that baptism in the Spirit is a very powerful event and is intimately linked with witness and missionary endeavour.

A fluid interpretation: A third option recognizes that in the New Testament the idea of the baptism of the Spirit is fuller than we realize. It is a fluid term that points to the life-changing reality of life in the Spirit of God. Sometimes it is used with overtones of regeneration (1 Corinthians 12:13); on other occasions it has overtones of spiritual empowering (Acts 1:5, 8). Basically it is a metaphor for the reality of new life and new power into which we are plunged when we are converted. It is an inclusive term, referring to the totality of spiritual reality that the Spirit begins in us and which is made available in the new age that began with Pentecost.

So it is difficult to use the term of only one part of the Spirit's work, and when we do so, we risk imbalance. Christian baptism speaks about the work of the Spirit. As we are plunged into the water, so we are plunged by Christ into the realm of the Spirit. It can be argued, therefore, that all Christians have been baptized in the Spirit (they have entered into new life) and also that all Christians need to be baptized in the Spirit (they need to enter into the experience of the Spirit's power). This may sound like saying that everybody is right. Actually it is saying that the truth about the Spirit is bigger than all of us. Those who disagree over this subject may well be stressing different aspects of the total truth.

The Spirit's 'coming'

Part of the problem of understanding the Spirit's work comes because we are too wooden in the way we think. This can be seen in the way in which the verb used in the New Testament is changed into a noun. The New Testament speaks of 'baptizing' in the Spirit, whereas we make this into the 'baptism' of the Spirit. In doing so, we risk making a dynamic work of God into a thing or an object over which we can contend. The Spirit of God is living, dynamic, moving. God's Spirit is sent out into the world to draw us through the Son to the Father. To enter into the Spirit's work is to become a part of this dynamic movement, to be caught up by the Spirit into God. We need to be cautious about defining the Spirit too closely. Jesus reminded us that the Spirit is like the wind and cannot be taken hold of (John 3:8). We may describe the Spirit's work but cannot define it. Whatever opinion we have, if we say 'this is how the Spirit works and if it isn't like this it can't be the Spirit', then we are trying to imprison the wind.

An alternative model for understanding might be to change the language and speak of the Spirit's 'coming'. The Spirit comes to people when they are first converted: this may be called the 'definitive' coming. But we need the Spirit to keep on coming to us, and therefore need to be open to the 'now' comings of the Spirit. Moreover, the comings of the Spirit may vary in intensity and from occasion to occasion. Christians are those to whom the Spirit of God has come, yet they are those to whom the dynamic Spirit of God keeps on coming, to renew, intensify, deepen and increase what was given from Christ in the Spirit's first coming. There is plenty of room for the continuing work of the Spirit after conversion, but there is never a movement beyond the Christ whom we have come to know in conversion. The Christian life is only ever an ongoing exploration of that which is mediated to us from God, in and through Jesus Christ. No Christian should doubt that there is always more of God in Christ into which the Spirit wants to bring us.

THE SPIRIT'S EQUIPPING WORK

The Spirit of God comes bringing gifts to enable us to serve. We have already examined this subject in some measure but some further comment is appropriate.

The responsibility for imparting gifts is the Spirit's. 'To each is given the manifestation of the Spirit for the common good' (1 Corinthians 12:7). In 1 Corinthians 12, Paul emphasizes the free, dynamic and spontaneous way in which the Spirit imparts whatever God wills, to whomever God wills, whenever God wills (vv. 7–11). Paul's point is that whatever the Spirit imparts is gift. No one has reason to boast or to imagine himself or herself superior to others, since we have nothing that we did not receive. The gifts that the Spirit brings, many and diverse as they are, are given so that the presence of Jesus Christ may be known as a reality within his body.

It is unhelpful to imagine that such gifts are solely vocal in nature. They include serving, helping and giving (Romans 12:7–8). They are the many and concrete ways in which Christ by his Spirit draws near through the people who are his. Spiritual gifts can therefore only be rightly employed in love (1 Corinthians 13).

The responsibility for using gifts is ours. Although the gifts are of the Spirit, the Spirit's action does not deprive individuals of responsible involvement in their use or manifestation. When Paul asserted that 'the spirits of prophets are subject to the prophets' (1 Corinthians 14:32), he no doubt did so because in the church at Corinth there were those who were claiming that the Spirit 'made them' prophesy in a way over which they had no control. Paul rejects this claim. We are responsible both for using what we have been given and for the ways in which we do so. Again, this makes sense of Paul's great chapter on love (1 Corinthians 13) in the midst of his discussion of the nature and use of spiritual gifts in the congregation (1 Corinthians 12—14).

THE SPIRIT'S INTERCEDING WORK

God's Spirit helps us to pray. Significant in this respect are Paul's words in Romans 8:26–27:

Likewise the Spirit helps us in our weakness; for we do not know how to pray as we ought, but that very Spirit intercedes for us with sighs too deep for words. And God, who searches the heart, knows what is the mind of the Spirit, because the Spirit intercedes for the saints according to the will of God.

Later in Romans 8, Paul also tells us that the Son of God prays for us (v. 34). Here he tells us that the Spirit of God, the divine current of communication between the Father and the Son, prays in us. When we know neither what to pray nor how to pray, the Spirit knows the will of God and, in ways deeper than words, interprets our inner longings to the Father.

The Spirit is therefore intimately involved with the activity of prayer and supports and undergirds us in our praying. Whereas we are inclined to think of prayer as a chore or a duty that must be performed, these words teach us that prayer is a gracious gift from God. It is not an activity that we initiate but one in which we join, since the Spirit is already praying to the Father. We should think of prayer as a conversation taking place within God, in which we are enabled to participate and to which we contribute by the Spirit of God. This is the conversation that we see taking place in Luke 10:21 and to which Jesus indicates, in 10:22–24, that we also will gain access. When we are conscious of the inadequacy of our prayers, these words speak of the help of the Spirit in making them adequate.

THE SPIRIT'S RESURRECTING WORK

The final aspect of the Spirit's work that we shall outline here concerns a future work that we have yet to see. As the Spirit was the means whereby Jesus was raised out of death (1 Peter 3:18), so the Spirit is the one through whom believers will be restored to full personal existence in a glorified form. We call this the resurrection: 'If the Spirit of him who raised Jesus from the dead dwells in you, he who raised Christ from the dead will give life to your mortal bodies also through his Spirit that dwells in you' (Romans 8:11).

How all this is to be passes our understanding. What it is like to live in a spiritual body (1 Corinthians 15:44), we do not know. We might, however, gain some clues from the resurrection of Jesus, whose physical body was both transformed and glorified while remaining recognizably the one that he possessed in his earthly life. Possibly, his body was still undergoing transformation during the resurrection appearances. It is fair to conclude that a similar transformation of believers will be accomplished by the Spirit, who will complete the work of which 1 Corinthians 15:49 speaks: 'Just as we have borne the image of the man of dust, we will also bear the image of the man of heaven.'

With this tentative examination of the resurrection we have almost completed our survey of the Spirit's work in the individual. In doing so, we stress once more the practical value of what we have considered. If the Spirit is so completely and intimately involved in fulfilling God's saving purposes in us, the only way we can live is in absolute dependence on God the Spirit for life, holiness, power, gifts, guidance and the future. Before we move on to the next chapter, however, a special note is warranted on that gift of the Spirit known as 'speaking in tongues'.

SPEAKING IN TONGUES

This topic has caused much contention ever since the rise of Pentecostalism and the charismatic movement, both of which have been strongly marked by the rediscovery of the gift and its manifestation in various ways, both in private prayer and in public ministry. There are those who object to it altogether in the belief that the manifestation of the gift was limited to the period of the early Church; others object to the importance that is ascribed to the gift and the ways it is interpreted and put to use.

As noted, on the Day of Pentecost the first community of disciples were 'filled with the Holy Spirit and began to speak in other languages, as the Spirit gave them ability' (Acts 2:4). After this, the phenomenon was explicitly repeated on two significant occasions: the so-called 'Gentile Pentecost' in Acts 10:46, and the conversion of the Ephesian disciples in Acts 19:6. It may be that the gift of tongues is also implied in the experience of the 'Samaritan Pentecost' in Acts 8:17–18. Apart from these occasions, tongues is the subject (along with other gifts) of an extended discussion in 1 Corinthians 12—14. The references to the gift in the book of Acts place it in the context of significant breakthroughs in the mission of the Church, first among the Jews of the diaspora, then (perhaps) among the Samaritans, the Gentiles and the Ephesians. The Corinthian correspondence, by contrast, is dealing with it in the more settled conditions of a local church, albeit one that is experiencing a degree of turbulence over the subject. A series of questions arises:

- What is the gift of tongues?
- Did not the gift of tongues cease?
- Is the gift of tongues the 'initial evidence' of being baptized in the Holy Spirit?
- How should the gift of tongues be practised?
- What about singing in the Spirit?

What is the gift of tongues?

Ostensibly, the references in Acts relate to a supra-normal ability to speak in known foreign languages and to make oneself understood. The astonished response on the part of the hearers is, 'And how is it that we hear, each of us, in our own native language?' (2:8). In Corinthians, however, things are less certain. Speaking in tongues is unintelligible unless accompanied by the exercise of a further supra-normal gift, that of interpretation (1 Corinthians 14:4–5).

The Corinthian experience corresponds more closely to contemporary charismatic experience, in which *glossolalia* (the Greek term which means speaking in languages or tongues) takes the form of 'ecstatic speech', a form of 'pre-conceptual' speech that flows from the inner life of the speaker as an expression of love and worship to God. This may be understood by analogy to spontaneous and improvised singing or playing of an instrument. It is also well established that it is a general human capacity, that it is not exclusive to Christians or even to religious believers, and that the areas of the brain that are operative during its use can be identified.

This should not be surprising, since all human experience has to engage the brain at some level to be even a possibility. It does mean, however, that what makes speaking in tongues a spiritual gift is not that it is 'supernatural' but that the Spirit of God claims and consecrates this aspect of human ability for a spiritual purpose. This, of course, is what the Spirit does with all other aspects of our human nature. It is not a question of the Spirit overriding human nature but of working with human nature to offer glory back to God. In this case, as with other gifts, it is in the depths of human intuition as distinct from intellect that the Spirit is at work—which is what Paul means when he says, 'For if I pray in a tongue, my spirit prays but my mind is unproductive' (1 Corinthians 14:14). This by no means invalidates the gift for Paul, but it does lead to the need for proper harmony of spirit and mind, of intuition and intellect: 'What should I do then? I will pray with the spirit, but I will pray with the mind also; I will sing praise with the spirit, but I will sing praise with the mind also' (1 Corinthians 14:15).

Despite the occasional anecdote to the contrary, hard and documented evidence is lacking that in the contemporary experience of tongues (widespread as it is) actual human languages are being employed. Paul's words in 1 Corinthians 13:1, 'If I speak in the tongues of mortals and of angels, but do not have love...' are to be taken rhetorically rather than analytically.

It may well be, then, that the phenomenon of tongues in Acts 2 is different from that in Corinthians, and that the contemporary gift is more akin to the Corinthian experience. The suggestion that the gift can be differentiated in this way is quite in accord with the reference to 'various kinds of tongues' in 1 Corinthians 12:28. It could also be, however, that the miracle of tongues in Acts 2 is not so much one of speaking as of hearing. In other words, when the witnesses of Pentecost proclaim, 'How is it that we hear, each of us, in our own native language' (2:8), the miracle is not that the apostles are speaking in actual foreign languages but that, while speaking in ecstatic speech, they are heard in the many languages of those who are witnessing the event, and that this is the work of the Spirit.

Did not the gift of tongues cease?

For many people, the discussion we have just had is an unnecessary one for the simple reason that the gift of tongues was never intended to be a permanent endowment on the Church. It was part of a number of phenomena that accompanied the early Church until the time when the New Testament scriptures were established as the Church's primary source of authority, after which it ceased. Consequently, all claims to manifest the gift today are self-deceiving and have their origin in human effort or (in the most extreme form of this argument) in the occult. Appeal is made to 1 Corinthians 13:8–11:

Love never ends. But as for prophecies, they will come to an end; as for tongues, they will cease; as for knowledge, it will come to an end. For we know only in part, and we prophesy only in part; but when the complete comes, the partial will come to an end. When I was a child, I spoke like a child, I thought like a child, I reasoned like a child; when I became an adult, I put an end to childish ways.

Of course, the argument only works if 'the complete' is understood to be the establishment of the New Testament canon. As it is, the passage is clearly referring to the time when we shall see Christ 'face to face' (v. 12), and this can only be a reference to Christ's final coming. In this case, the force of the passage is the precise opposite of what is claimed. Tongues and prophecy continue until the time of Christ's coming and only then should they be put away. The childish immaturities which are here in view are not the exercise of spiritual gifts, but the conflicts surrounding them that were taking place in the Church and needed to be overcome.

The greatest flaw in the 'cessationist' argument is the assumption that the Christian life as we now know it, without many of the spiritual gifts, is normal, whereas the experience of the first Christians, with the gifts, was abnormal. If anything is true, surely it is the opposite: that the church has frequently declined from its good beginnings into a state of apathy and emptiness, whereas the New Testament church was on fire with the Holy Spirit. There is clearly some validity in the argument that the experiences of the first believers were unique and distinctive, accompanied by intense spiritual activity, but this is no reason to deny that their experiences of spiritual gifts continued in the Church in succeeding generations, or that the Lord of the Church is able to bestow whichever gifts he chooses upon it at whatever point.

Is the gift of tongues the 'initial evidence' of being baptized in the Holy Spirit?

We have already noted the flexible nature of the metaphor of being baptized in the Spirit. Believers who have received the Holy Spirit in their conversion still need to go on being baptized in the Holy Spirit. This is best seen not as a second crisis experience but as a continual need that all of us have, just as we need to be continually baptized in the love of God.

In some Pentecostal circles in which baptism of the Spirit is seen as a second crisis experience, tongues is sometimes described as the 'initial evidence' of it. This belief is based upon those experiences in the book of Acts in which the coming of the Spirit is accompanied by tongues. The danger of such a claim is that of prescribing how the Spirit's coming needs to be authenticated, and therefore of pressing everybody's experience into the same mould. As we have noted, the Spirit is unpredictable, like the wind, and infinitely creative.

Moreover, we should not compare ourselves with other people in such a way as to imagine that their gifts need to be our gifts. This is the essence of Paul's argument in 1 Corinthians 12:18–20: 'But as it is, God arranged the members in the body, each one of them, as he chose. If all were a single member, where would the body be? As it is, there are many members, yet one body.' Receiving the gift of tongues may well be, for some, a moment of spiritual renewal and new assurance of being a child of God. But to press this understanding upon everybody is to make a gracious gift into a necessary law and so to do violence to the very nature of spiritual gifts as gifts. It is far better to acknowledge the varieties of the Spirit's working and let God be God.

How should the gift of tongues be practised?

The use of the gift of tongues is both personal and public in nature. When used in private, it acts as a supplement to a believer's prayer life, a way of uttering mysteries to God and a means of building oneself up by means of deepening communion with God (1 Corinthians 14:4). Something deeper and more complete than mental activity on its own is taking place. This should be seen as the primary purpose of the gift. Yet those who use it in this way should also pray for the ability to interpret their own prayers, in order to inform their minds as well as building up their spirits and so to be further enriched (1 Corinthians 14:13–14).

We might imagine that an interpretation of prayer to God in tongues will take the form of prayer addressed in a Godward direction. But Paul envisages another use of tongues in the form of an address *to* the people of God. In this case, tongues followed by interpretation becomes the equivalent of prophecy. Paul gives particular value to prophecy as a means of building up the church:

Those who speak in a tongue build up themselves, but those who prophesy build up the church. Now I would like all of you to speak in tongues, but even more to prophesy. One who prophesies is greater than one who speaks in tongues, unless someone interprets, so that the church may be built up... I thank God that I speak in tongues more than all of you; nevertheless, in church I would rather speak five words with my mind, in order to instruct others also, than ten thousand words in a tongue.
1 CORINTHIANS 14:4–5, 18–19

At first it seems odd that a message should take the form of a tongue which then needs interpretation. If it is the interpretation that counts, why does Paul not simply encourage more prophecy by eliminating the tongue? Those who do find this somewhat odd need to remember that this is part of the New Testament scriptures and not just some charismatic fad, lately invented. Perhaps what the tongue adds is a sense of mystery, of the divine presence accompanied by an appropriate sense of awe. The interpretation makes sense of a mysterious moment in the gathering for worship and enables the mind to be fruitful as well. Also, it is an interpretation rather than a translation: the interpreter expresses at an intelligible but still intuitive level what a tongue expresses from the depths of a person's communion with God.

What about singing in the Spirit?

Many charismatic churches allow times of free praise within their worship, when the worshippers improvise their own words and melodies of worship, usually in creative harmonies that can be very beautiful. It is unclear whether or not this is what Paul had in mind when he wrote:

I will pray with the spirit, but I will pray with the mind also; I will sing praise with the spirit; but I will sing praise with the mind also. Otherwise, if you say a blessing with the spirit, how can anyone in the position of an outsider say the 'Amen' to your thanksgiving, since the outsider does not know what you are saying? For you may give thanks well enough, but the other person is not built up.

1 CORINTHIANS 14:15–17

Some argue that singing in tongues in worship should not be permitted since there is no interpretation. Just as praying in the Spirit and praying in tongues are not necessarily the same thing, however (Ephesians 6:18), so free praise in the Spirit is likely to involve not only the use of tongues but also of ordinary speech and language. This might be seen as interpretation of the tongues employed. When such praise is led well, it is good for those who are leading to offer intelligible prayer in which the singing in the Spirit and in tongues is summed up for the benefit of all.

It is disproportionate to spend so much time on a gift that the apostle Paul is anxious to de-emphasize in importance, but this is a sign of the debates that have arisen around the gift in recent years. It is to be hoped that the debates are now being seen in more measured and modest perspectives.

Chapter 8

THE SPIRIT AND THE FUTURE

The final aspect of our study is possibly the most difficult, since it concerns what is yet to be. We have prepared for this by considering the Spirit's work in resurrection. The resurrection of Jesus represents the entry into history of the glorious future that awaits us. In his victory over death, Christ is 'the first fruits of those who have died' (1 Corinthians 15:20). The Spirit who raised Christ from death is also the one through whom we will be raised from death (Romans 8:11). We can hardly imagine how this will be, although the fact that Jesus has already been raised helps us.

In this chapter, we go on to make the claim that the future belongs to the Spirit. It is as though the Spirit is the power of the future at work in the present. It is significant that, in the Creed, faith in the Holy Spirit as the life-giver is confessed in the same section as the life everlasting. The Spirit is the forward thrust who draws the whole of creation to its ultimate goal of unification in Christ and submission to the Father (Ephesians 1:10; 1 Corinthians 15:28).

THE SPIRIT AND THE TEMPLE

Something of this kind is already implied by the image of the temple. 1 Corinthians 3:16 makes it clear that the Church and the temple are closely associated: 'Do you not know that you are God's temple and that God's Spirit dwells in you?' The idea that God has a dwelling place develops throughout the Bible and can be seen as a key motif that comes to be played in different ways as the symphony of scripture unfolds. It will be worth tracing this theme in order to make the point.

The tabernacle

The fact that God desires a dwelling place is made clear to the children of Israel as they emerge from slavery in Egypt and make their way to the promised land. They are given detailed instructions to build a 'tent of meeting' and to furnish it in particular ways (Exodus 25—31; 37—40). When all of this is done, the Lord takes up residence in the tabernacle:

Then the cloud covered the tent of meeting, and the glory of the Lord filled the tabernacle. Moses was not able to enter the tent of meeting because the cloud settled upon it, and the glory of the Lord filled the tabernacle. Whenever the cloud was taken up from the tabernacle, the Israelites would set out on each stage of their journey; but if the cloud was not taken up, then they did not set out until the day that it was taken up. For the cloud of the Lord was on the tabernacle by day, and fire was in the cloud by night, before the eyes of all the house of Israel at each stage of their journey.
EXODUS 40:34–38

The cloud here, as frequently in scripture, symbolizes God's presence among the people; God's glory goes out from God's own self to be present in the tabernacle as an extension of himself. In this we can see the power of the Spirit of God at work in the world, and especially the desire of God to draw near. In the tabernacle, the people of Israel were able to draw near to God in their turn, to offer sacrifices and worship.

God's presence was also symbolized by the ark of the covenant, which was understood as God's throne and was placed in the holy of holies, the inner sanctum and most holy place of the tabernacle (Exodus 25:10–22). Here the high priest would offer sacrifices on the day of Atonement each year (Leviticus 16).

The temple

In time, once Israel had settled in the land of Canaan and had taken possession of the city of Jerusalem, the tabernacle was replaced by a temple, built in the reign of King Solomon. The ark of the covenant was moved into the temple (2 Chronicles 5:2–10), and we read that as the priests sang to God at the consecration of the temple, 'the house, the house of the Lord, was filled with a cloud, so that the priests could not stand to minister because of the cloud; for the glory of the Lord filled the house of God' (2 Chronicles 5:13–14).

The temple was the dwelling place of God, the place where his glory was made known (Ezekiel 10:4; Haggai 2:9). As the tabernacle had been, so the temple was the central place of Israel's worship, the place of sacrifice and of encounter with God. The temple passed through various episodes in which it was destroyed and rebuilt, desecrated and reconsecrated at the time of the Maccabees, and then replaced entirely at the time of King Herod with a fabulous new structure that is generally referred to as the 'second temple'. This was the building destroyed by the Romans in AD70, as foreseen and predicted by Jesus (Matthew 24:1–2).

Jesus and the temple

A crucial stage in the temple theme is reached with the incarnation. In Jesus Christ, the dwelling place of God among human beings became a living person of whom it could be said, 'And the Word became flesh and lived among us, and we have seen his glory, the glory as of a father's only son, full of grace and truth' (John 1:14).

Jesus seems to have understood himself as a replacement for the physical temple in Jerusalem. As he was in debate with the Jewish leaders of his day, we read:

Jesus answered them, 'Destroy this temple, and in three days I will raise it up.' The Jews then said, 'This temple has been under construction for forty-

six years, and will you raise it up in three days?' But he was speaking of
the temple of his body. After he was raised from the dead, his disciples
remembered that he had said this; and they believed the scripture and the
word that Jesus had spoken.

JOHN 2:19–22

As the temple had been the central place of worship, so Christians
are to see Jesus Christ as the one in whom God has made his
dwelling in our midst and who now stands at the centre of our
access to God. He is both God drawing near in an ultimate sense
and the means of our drawing near to God through him and
through the sacrificial offering of his life on the cross. But Jesus was
on this earth only for a certain period. After his death, resurrection
and ascension, the focus changes once more.

The Church as the temple

After the ascension, it is the Church that becomes the temple in
which the Spirit lives. The location of God's dwelling with humankind was moved from being a tent to being a building, then to being
a person, and then to being a community. Jesus promised that he
would build his Church (Matthew 16:18), and Paul saw the Church
in this way:

For through [Christ] both of us have access in one Spirit to the Father.
So then you are no longer strangers and aliens, but you are citizens
with the saints and also members of the household of God, built upon
the foundation of the apostles and prophets, with Christ himself as the
cornerstone. In him the whole structure is joined together and grows into
a holy temple in the Lord; in whom you also are built together spiritually
into a dwelling-place for God.

EPHESIANS 2:18–22

The Father and the Son have made their dwelling in the Church
by the Holy Spirit. Each Christian is a temple of the Holy Spirit

(1 Corinthians 3:16–17). Christians are like 'living stones', so Peter says, 'Let yourselves be built into a spiritual house, to be a holy priesthood, to offer spiritual sacrifices acceptable to God through Jesus Christ' (1 Peter 2:5).

All creation as the final temple

All of this is, of course, a prelude to the day which is the hope of all creation, the day when the whole of creation becomes the dwelling place, the temple, of God. This is the day gloriously anticipated in the book of Revelation:

And I saw the holy city, the new Jerusalem, coming down out of heaven from God, prepared as a bride adorned for her husband. And I heard a loud voice from the throne saying, 'See, the home of God is among mortals. He will dwell with them; they will be his peoples, and God himself will be with them; he will wipe every tear from their eyes. Death will be no more; mourning and crying and pain will be no more, for the first things have passed away.'
REVELATION 21:2–4

In this chapter, the city of God is portrayed as a cube (v. 16), in the same way that the holy of holies in the Jerusalem temple was a cube (1 Kings 6:20; 2 Chronicles 3:8–9). In the symbolism of Revelation, this means that God is now fully present throughout his creation and not just in limited parts of it. For this reason, the city portrayed is large and capacious enough to contain all who wish to be part of it, and also the treasures and wealth of earth. It is translucent, and so shines with the light and glory of God that there is no need for sun or moon 'for the glory of God is its light, and its lamp is the Lamb' (Revelation 21:23).

This chapter is a vision of the day when God will be 'all in all' (1 Corinthians 15:28). No longer to be associated only with parts of the created order (the tabernacle and temple, the Christ or the

Church), God now fills all things. This is the expansive drama of the scriptures, which portrays the movement of God outwards by the Spirit as God searches for a dwelling place. God's ultimate goal is that 'the earth will be filled with the knowledge of the glory of the Lord, as the waters cover the sea' (Habakkuk 2:14).

THE SPIRIT'S FORWARD THRUST

This goal of God may be understood as follows. It is biblical and traditional to think of the Spirit as coming into the world from the Father through the Son (Father > Son > Spirit). With the gift of the Spirit, however, we find a pivot on which the whole of the world turns. After Pentecost, the Spirit furthers the work of salvation by restoring all things through Christ to the Father (Spirit > Son > Father). The Spirit comes to us through the Son in order that through the Son the same Spirit might restore the world to the Father. This work will be accomplished only in the fullness of time and is looked forward to as 'the time of universal restoration that God announced long ago through his holy prophets' (Acts 3:21).

The prophets speak of this time in many different ways. Isaiah, for example, pictures it like this:

The wolf shall live with the lamb, the leopard shall lie down with the kid, the calf and the lion and the fatling together, and a little child shall lead them. The cow and the bear shall graze, their young shall lie down together; and the lion shall eat straw like the ox. The nursing child shall play over the hole of the asp, and the weaned child shall put its hand on the adder's den. They will not hurt or destroy on all my holy mountain; for the earth will be full of the knowledge of the Lord as the waters cover the sea.
ISAIAH 11:6–9

It will be the age when life-giving water will flow into all the world, bringing fruitfulness and healing (Ezekiel 47), when darkness will be abolished and the Lord's name will be the only name worshipped (Zechariah 14:6–9). With many glorious images and signposts, the prophets point us forward to a time when conflict and fear will be abolished and the world will be transformed into an ultimate harmony in Father, Son and Holy Spirit. This is the time of final peace. It is the time of the new heaven and new earth in which righteousness dwells (Isaiah 65:17; 2 Peter 3:13).

The fact that it is the Spirit's particular work to draw all things towards this ultimate goal may be generally understood from all that we have previously said about the Spirit. As the Spirit at work in creating the world and in recreating the Church in the image of Christ, he is the active presence of God, bringing God's purposes to pass. Specifically, the Spirit is related to this future age in Joel 2:28–32. The pouring out of the Spirit on all flesh is here linked to 'the great and terrible day of the Lord' (v. 31) with its attendant upheavals in the created sphere, which are signs of the 'earth-shattering' transformation that creation is to undergo.

Peter sees Joel's prophecy to be in process of fulfilment on the day of Pentecost (Acts 2:16–21). The point he makes is that the Spirit who is associated with the final day of the Lord has actually come in the here and now to bring salvation. This corresponds to Paul's teaching about the Spirit as a down-payment of what is to come: 'But it is God who establishes us with you in Christ and has anointed us, by putting his seal on us and giving us his Spirit in our hearts as a first instalment' (2 Corinthians 1:21–22; see also 5:5).

Similarly, Paul says, 'In him you also, when you had heard the word of truth, the gospel of your salvation, and had believed in him, were marked with the seal of the promised Holy Spirit; this is the pledge of our inheritance towards redemption as God's own people, to the praise of his glory' (Ephesians 1:13–14).

The knowledge of the Spirit who creates communion by binding things together is a foretaste of the final unification of all things by the Spirit in the Son with the Father.

THE SPIRIT AS 'TRANS-CREATOR'

One way of expressing this aspect of the Spirit's work is to see the Spirit as the 'Trans-creator'. Because the Spirit is involved in creation, it is right to see him as Creator-Spirit. Because the Spirit renews us in the image of Christ, it is also right to see him as the Recreator-Spirit. He is also the Trans-creator in that through him the world is being transformed towards its ultimate goal in Christ. The Spirit is the one who is crossing the gaps and who will one day close the gap of alienation in the world to restore all things to the Father. In this trans-creative work, we see the Spirit making for the fellowship of all things with the Father through the Son. This is the ultimate salvation for which we hope and of which we have the 'deposit'.

Of course, this work of the Spirit needs to be seen in intimate connection with the Father and the Son as they work together for the fulfilment of the divine purpose. In the Introduction, we made reference to the difference of opinion about the Spirit which led to the division of East and West in 1054 and which centred on the so-called *filioque* clause in the Creed. This may seem a trivial debate, but behind it are some large issues of theological principle. The Eastern Church was concerned that by describing the Spirit in this way (as proceeding 'from the Father *and from the Son*'), the Spirit was being situated in third place in the life of God and therefore devalued: the Spirit was derived from the Father and the Son, but neither other person of the Trinity was derived from the Spirit. Did this make the Spirit inferior? Yet to describe the Spirit as proceeding from the Father and from the Son marks the Spirit out as the Spirit of the Son, to be recognized as being at work only in so far as he brings to pass whatever honours and glorifies Jesus Christ.

In turn, this becomes a way in which we may discern whether something is truly of God or not. The Spirit is not to be found in any and every supposedly spiritual experience but only in those that lead to personal confession of Christ (1 John 4:3) and to the kind of living that is consistent with him. It is in the light of Christ that we recognize what is of the Spirit of Christ, just as surely as it is through the Spirit that our eyes are opened to Christ.

In order to be true both to the wider work of the Spirit in creation, history and salvation, which we have sought to stress, and to the intimacy of the link between Christ and the Spirit, we might think of trying to improve on the Nicene Creed. This might be attempted (were it permitted) by affirming that the Son of God is 'eternally begotten of the Father *through the Spirit*' and by confessing the belief in 'the Holy Spirit who proceeds from the Father *through the Son*'. The first of these formulae does greater justice to the work of the Spirit in the incarnation of Christ and sees this work as the expression of an eternal involvement of the Spirit of God in the being of the Son. The second acknowledges that the Spirit comes to us through Jesus and is to be recognized by reference to him and to none other. In this way, the statements about the Holy Spirit are enhanced without taking away from the strong statements about the Son.

We shall conclude this discussion on the Spirit and the future by showing the perspectives to which it leads us: on ourselves, on the Church and on the world.

A PERSPECTIVE ON OURSELVES

Because we are those who have received the Spirit, we are those who have entered, in the here and now, into the peace that will one day be shared by the whole creation (Romans 8:18–25). The Holy Spirit has been poured into our hearts, bringing confident hope that one day all creation will be at peace.

A PERSPECTIVE ON THE CHURCH

The Church is the community of the Spirit that is in the world now as a sign of the ultimate reconciliation of all things (Ephesians

2:14–22). The Spirit is already making us into the kind of community that will inherit the earth. The Church lives in the Spirit. It anticipates the reunion of all humanity in Christ (Matthew 8:11). It shares together in the feast of bread and wine which is a foretaste of the recreation of the heavens and the earth (Matthew 26:29; Revelation 19:9, 17). It lives not according to the pattern of the alienated world in this age, but in love and justice according to the power of the age that will be (Romans 12:1–2). In these ways, the Church is the sign and agent of the future, the pioneer of a way of living that will one day be vindicated by events.

A PERSPECTIVE ON THE WORLD

As the world has its being in the Spirit, we are entitled to see the Spirit at work beyond the confines of the Church in every act of humanity, every movement towards a more just, Christ-like existence, everything that is good and fine, gathering all things together and drawing them forward to the restoration of all things. While the Spirit is at work first and foremost and explicitly in the Church, he is also at work implicitly in everything that harmonizes with Christ in the world at large. All good things come from God, wherever they are found. The hidden providence of God is at work all around us.

This is one of the bases on which Christians should involve themselves in all that makes for justice and peace, believing that in doing so they are working together with God the Spirit towards the day of final redemption. To have this perspective is a constant reminder that the Lord who is the Spirit is present throughout the creation.

In Revelation 22 we are given another glimpse of the end of all things and of God's final victory. We read:

Then the angel showed me the river of the water of life, bright as crystal, flowing from the throne of God and of the Lamb through the middle of

the street of the city. On either side of the river is the tree of life with its
twelve kinds of fruit, producing its fruit each month; and the leaves of the
tree are for the healing of the nations.
REVELATION 22:1–2

In this vision, the crystal river represents the Spirit. Wherever the
river flows, it brings life, healing and abundance. The warfare of the
nations and their ancient scars are healed because of the life-giving
water. So it is with the Spirit, who flows to us from the Father
through the Son to bring all things to their ultimate and glorious
goal in the knowledge of God. So not only the prophecies of
scripture but the longings of our hearts and of the whole creation
find their fulfilment in the eternal presence and communion of the
ever-living God, Father, Son and Spirit.

CONCLUSION

We began this book with the intention of testing against scripture
the Church's existing conclusion that the Holy Spirit is both truly
personal and truly God. The evidence we have examined bears this
out. According to Christian faith, therefore, the Holy Spirit is to be
honoured and adored in union with the Father and the Son as God.
In the words of the Nicene Creed, 'I believe in the Holy Spirit...
who with the Father and the Son together is to be worshipped and
glorified.'

To honour the Holy Spirit is not purely a matter of theology.
Where the Spirit is most honoured, the Spirit is most free to fulfil
the mission of glorifying Jesus Christ in the lives of those who
believe, drawing them to the Father through him. It is not simply
correct but of vital importance to the well-being of the Church that
the Spirit should receive the rightful place in our thinking, our
worship and our lives. The words of the hymn are appropriate:

All praise to God the Father be,
All praise, eternal Son to Thee,
Whom with the Spirit we adore,
For ever and for evermore. Amen.

FURTHER READING

Harvey Cox, *Fire from Heaven: The Rise of Pentecostal Spirituality and the Reshaping of Religion in the Twenty-First Century* (Cassell, 1996)

James Dunn, *Jesus and the Spirit: A Study of the Religious and Charismatic Experience of Jesus and the First Christians as Reflected in the New Testament* (SCM Press, 1975)

Michael Eaton, *Baptism with the Spirit: The Teaching of Martyn Lloyd-Jones* (IVP, 1989)

Paul Fiddes, *Charismatic Renewal: A Baptist View* (Baptist Union, 1975)

Michael Green, *I Believe in the Holy Spirit* (Hodder and Stoughton, 1975)

Colin Gunton, *The Promise of Trinitarian Theology* (T&T Clark, 1991)

Alasdair Heron, *The Holy Spirit in the Bible, in the History of Christian Thought and in Recent Theology* (Marshall, Morgan and Scott, 1977)

Morton Kelsey, *Tongue Speaking: An Experiment in Spiritual Experience* (Hodder and Stoughton, 1968)

Jürgen Moltmann, *The Church in the Power of the Holy Spirit* (SCM Press, 1977)

J.I. Packer, *Keep in Step with the Spirit* (IVP, 1984)

Philip J. Rosato, *The Spirit as Lord: The Pneumatology of Karl Barth* (T&T Clark, 1981)

Philip J. Rosato, 'The Holy Spirit' in *A New Dictionary of Christian Theology* edited by Alan Richardson and John Bowden (SCM Press, 1983)

John Ruthven, *On the Cessation of the Charismata: The Protestant Polemic on Postbiblical Miracles* (Sheffield Academic Press, 1993)

Thomas Smail, *Reflected Glory: The Spirit in Christ and Christians* (Hodder and Stoughton, 1975)

Thomas Smail, *The Giving Gift: The Holy Spirit in Person* (Hodder and Stoughton, 1988)

Thomas Smail, Andrew Walker and Nigel Wright, *Charismatic Renewal: The Search for a Theology* (SPCK, 1995)

John Taylor, *The Go-Between God: The Holy Spirit and the Christian Mission* (SCM Press, 1972)

QUESTIONS FOR DISCUSSION

INTRODUCTION

1. How do you respond to the idea that the Holy Spirit has been neglected? Is this true of the teaching you have received? In what ways might you personally have neglected the Spirit?
2. Are there any other reasons you can think of why the Spirit may have been neglected?
3. What is it that has sparked your own interest in the Spirit and led you to read this book? Has what you have read so far added to that interest?
4. In this introductory part of your study, make a list of the questions you would like to have answered. If you find answers given in this book, revise your list and then see what remains.

CHAPTER 1: THE SPIRIT ON THE INSIDE

1. Reflect upon the words contained in the Nicene Creed about the Holy Spirit. How far do they accord with your own beliefs? What do you find puzzling or hard to believe?
2. This chapter puts a strong emphasis on the Spirit as the creator of fellowship. How true do you think this is to scripture?
3. What are the implications of saying that the Spirit is God? How does this affect (a) your own attitude to the Spirit; (b) your church's attitude?
4. Can you think of any hymns or songs that reflect the divinity and/or the personhood of the Spirit?

CHAPTER 2: THE SPIRIT AND CREATION

1. This chapter claims that many Christians have too small a vision of the Spirit. How does it propose to increase this vision?
2. What difference does it make to your zest for life to believe that the Spirit is so closely at work in creation?
3. How and when might it be possible to see the Spirit at work in the realm of politics? Can you think of any specific evidences of the Spirit's influence?
4. How does this chapter affect the way you think about (a) manual crafts and skills; (b) art; (c) music?

CHAPTER 3: THE SPIRIT AND REVELATION

1. How do you imagine that the gift of prophecy might function today? How can we discern the difference between true and false prophecy?
2. What does it mean to say that 'your sons and daughters will prophesy'? Are there implications in this for the community of men and women in the Church?
3. Can you think of any times when the Spirit has illuminated your reading of the Bible? How often does it happen?
4. Why is it that so many people appear not to understand or to receive the Christian gospel?

CHAPTER 4: THE SPIRIT AS THE GIVER OF JESUS

1. Does this chapter lead you to think in any new ways about the Spirit?
2. How would you express in your own words the role of the Spirit in giving Jesus to this world?

3. What is the link between the Spirit and the mighty works done by Jesus in his ministry? To what extent would it be true to say that Jesus was fully dependent on the Spirit of God?

4. How is the Spirit's distinctive work of creating fellowship expressed in the ministry of Jesus?

CHAPTER 5: THE SPIRIT AS THE GIFT OF JESUS

1. How would you understand the term 'baptism of the Holy Spirit'?

2. What was new about what happened on the day of Pentecost?

3. What are the implications of saying that the Spirit glorifies Jesus for your understanding of what the Spirit does in our own lives? How should Spirit-filled people live?

4. What things have been gained in the Church through the charismatic movement? Is there a down-side?

CHAPTER 6: THE SPIRIT AND THE CHURCH

1. Reflect upon what it means to say that the Church is the 'community of the Spirit'. How helpful a description is this? How is it expressed?

2. In what sense is the Spirit the Spirit of 'the end-time'? Does this mean that the Spirit comes to realize the purposes of God in the world? How is this done?

3. What do you think about the present-day use of spiritual gifts? Can you describe what the individual gifts listed in 1 Corinthians 12 are meant to accomplish? What does Paul mean in practical terms when he talks about building up the Church in 1 Corinthians 14?

4. What is the link between the Spirit and the mission of the Church? How possible is it for a church without a sense of mission to call itself a Spirit-filled church?

CHAPTER 7: THE SPIRIT AND THE BELIEVER

1. This chapter makes a link between what the Spirit did in Christ and what the Spirit does in believers. Do you feel that this brings us closer to Christ?
2. Can you identify any time at which you were 'convicted' of sin? How would you describe such an experience in your own language?
3. Can you think of times at which you experienced the assurance of the Holy Spirit? What were you being assured about?
4. In what ways is adoption as a child of God *greater* than being put right with God through repentance and faith?

CHAPTER 8: THE SPIRIT AND THE FUTURE

1. What pictures and images would you use to describe the future that God has planned for 'all things'?
2. How is God's Spirit engaged in realizing this future?
3. Would it be true or helpful to describe the Spirit (among other things) as the 'Spirit of the future'?
4. Does the coming of God's future depend in any way on the quality of our response to God? What does it mean to 'hasten' the day of the Lord or 'speed its coming' (2 Peter 3:12)?

brf

Resourcing your spiritual journey

through...

* Bible reading notes
* Books for Advent & Lent
* Books for Bible study and prayer
* Books to resource those working with under 11s in school, church and at home

* Quiet days and retreats
* Training for primary teachers and children's leaders
* Godly Play
* Barnabas Live

For more information, visit the **brf** website at **www.brf.org.uk**